Summary
Justice

Summary
Justice

Are Magistrates Up To It?

ROGER FARRINGTON

Matador
9 Priory Business Park,
Wistow Road, Kibworth Beauchamp,
Leicestershire. LE8 0RX
Tel: 0116 279 2299
Email: books@troubador.co.uk
Web: www.troubador.co.uk/matador
Twitter: @matadorbooks

ISBN 978 1785891 045

British Library Cataloguing in Publication Data.
A catalogue record for this book is available from the British Library.

Printed and bound by CPI Group (UK) Ltd, Croydon, CR0 4YY
Typeset in 11pt Minion Pro by Troubador Publishing Ltd, Leicester, UK

Matador is an imprint of Troubador Publishing Ltd

For Tricia Pank

Contents

Foreword

In June 2015, Mr. Michael Gove, Justice Secretary and Lord Chancellor in the freshly elected Conservative government, made a speech which received much attention. It conveyed his first impressions of how things were. There was much that he found unsatisfactory: the justice system was archaic and cumbersome, with 'snowdrifts of paper', 'indefensible' waste and 'grotesque inefficiencies'. There was a balancing recognition of what was admirable: 'the reputation of our independent judiciary... and the total absence of corruption in our courts and tribunals'. His view of the legal profession was notably complimentary. The speech was well received. Many of his criticisms echoed those made from time to time, and trenchantly, by senior members of the judiciary. There appears to be something approaching concurrence in his broad appraisal. This is encouraging for someone concerned to advocate some degree of change.

Gove's criticisms bore on the whole judicial system, civil as well as criminal. The scope of this book is much more restricted. It is with the process of summary justice in the criminal courts of England and Wales – that is, with the justice meted out by magistrates and district judges, sitting without a jury. It is addressed in the first place to the general reader – that is, to members of the public who wish to understand how magistrates' courts dispose of their business, and to judge how well they do it. It is addressed also to those whose interest is professional- magistrates themselves, lawyers, probation officers, court staff, journalists and others – to those considering applying for appointment as lay magistrates, and to students of law and criminology. It is also addressed to policy-makers, and I conclude with some proposals for change.

My perspective is that of someone engaged in the process, in this case from a seat on the bench. I served for twenty years as a justice of the peace – a lay magistrate – and throughout that period I kept a record of my sittings in court. I draw largely on this record in describing what happens, in the hope that this will give what I say an immediacy not otherwise obtainable. There should be no breach of confidence in this, as nearly all of what I deal with is well in the past, and no one will be identifiable. Both in the record and in what I now have to say about it, I seek to explain as well as to describe and to reflect on what I found perplexing and unsatisfactory. My discussion extends to the points of principle which are bound to come to the minds of those concerned and to observers.

I give some account of the origins and history of the magistracy, both lay and professional. I consider the present standing of the lay magistracy, and offer an appraisal of its effectiveness. I consider how this effectiveness might be enhanced. My object throughout is to bring out both how things are and how they might be. I conclude that the system is passably effective as it is, but that it could be made more effective to the general advantage. I conclude by presenting what I take to be the best way to bring this improvement about.

A Note on Terms

My use of terms in what follows may be confusing. I will often speak of 'the bench'. The word also refers to judges, but I am concerned here only with its application to magistrates. In that context 'the bench' may mean the magistracy as a whole ('to be appointed to the bench in the nineteenth century you needed to be well-connected'). It may also mean the total of the magistrates of any one place ('the Hull bench is about a hundred strong'). It may also mean the magistrates, usually two or three in number, sitting in court and doing the work ('the bench found him Guilty'). It may of course mean the piece of furniture which once supported all three of these meanings, but that is unlikely. Benches have gone, and the modern magistrate sits in a chair.

The word 'magistrate' itself also has several uses. Until quite recently, it covered both 'justice of the peace' or 'JP' - or 'lay magistrate' (the same thing) - and 'stipendiary magistrate'. Stipendiary magistrates are now styled 'district judges', and we no longer need to speak of 'lay magistrates' to bring out the difference. I have however sometimes found it convenient to do so. The distinction and how it came about is covered more fully in Chapter One below. Justices of the peace and district judges sit in the same court-houses, called 'magistrates' courts'.

In using the word 'summary' I do not exclude the familiar sense – that of prompt and brisk – but I normally have in mind a stricter sense, that of justice delivered by magistrates, or a single magistrate – a district judge - by themselves without juries.

HOW IT WORKS NOW

1.

The View from the Gallery

First impressions are often the most striking. Let us imagine someone who has never been in a court of law, who now walks into a magistrates' courthouse in a large conurbation. This might have been because he or she had to be there, either in response to a summons to attend, or because he or she had been arrested and then bailed to attend. It might also have been because he – suppose it is a man – had been asked to appear as a witness at the trial of someone else. In either case, he should have had some idea what to expect. Let us, however, suppose that our observer is neither of these and that he is prompted only by curiosity. Let us suppose also that the business conducted here concerns persons over the age of eighteen and is made up largely of alleged breaches of criminal law. There will then be a right to observe proceedings, which does not extend to the youth court or at the family proceedings court, where the presumption in favour of doing justice openly is over-ridden by the need for privacy.

If our supposed observer gives himself a week to sit and observe, and stays each day, from start to finish, he will come to appreciate the variety of magistrates' business. In the space of a week there is likely be a trial, or several, which might last for a day or two or for no more than half an hour. The procedure is very much what it would have been in the Crown Court, and this may be familiar to him through popular fiction or television. The important difference from the Crown Court is that the verdict – Guilty or

Not Guilty – is determined, not by a jury, for there is none, but by a bench of two or three lay magistrates, or possibly by one person sitting solo. If the verdict is Guilty, the defendant, now 'the offender', may be sentenced there or then, or the tribunal (whether one, two or three) may adjourn for a probation officer's report on him. They will hear what he or his legal representative, if he has one, has to say before passing sentence or deciding anything else.

Our observer may be surprised to find that magistrates do much more than preside over trials. He may sit through several busy mornings where a succession of defendants goes through the dock, perhaps twenty or thirty or more. These are likely to be people appearing for the first time, either after receiving a summons to attend or after being arrested and then bailed by the police to appear. There will be some who, for some reason, were not bailed and who are now brought to court from the prison to which they were remanded. They will usually be invited to plead to a charge, or more than one, which the clerk will read out. If the plea is Guilty, they may or may not be sentenced there and then. If it is Not Guilty, arrangements for a trial will be made. The date of this trial will often be weeks or several months into the future. It will then be a question whether a defendant awaiting trial can be given bail, with or without conditions attached to it, or whether he should be remanded in custody. The magistrates will hear any objections to bail which the prosecutor may put forward and then the defendant's or his representative's response.

Sometimes no plea will be taken at this stage, usually because the defendant, who very probably knows nothing of the law, wants to consult a lawyer before entering a plea. The judge or magistrate presiding will often encourage him or her to do this. A duty solicitor, a lawyer paid from public funds but independent of the court, should be available to advise him. It is up to the defendant to see the duty solicitor or to ask for an adjournment, so that he may go to a solicitor of his own choice.

Sometimes the offence with which a defendant appearing for the first time is charged is so serious that it can only be dealt with at the Crown Court and the magistrates' role is limited to sending it there. Sometimes it is for the magistrates to decide whether their court or the Crown Court should deal with a case, and they will do so after hearing a summary account of the supposed facts from the prosecutor and any representations from the prosecutor or the defence. Some of those who appear now will have appeared at an earlier hearing and either pleaded Guilty or been convicted after a trial. Where a probation officer's report on them was then commissioned, it will now be for the magistrates to pass sentence, taking account of the report and hearing what the defendant or his representative has to say.

All this is likely to be found interesting, at least to those coming to it afresh. Much else that happens is far from interesting, at least to the casual observer. Magistrates spend much of their time disposing of cases where the defendant is charged with one or more motoring offences. The charges are normally proved in their absence; the offenders are then required to appear in court on a later date if their disqualification from driving has to be considered. TV license evasion charges are dealt with in the same way. Only a small proportion of those charged will attend and once the magistrate presiding or the clerk has explained that it is an offence to watch television without a license very few will contest the charge. The remainder will, almost inevitably, be convicted in their absence once the prosecutor has given a summary account of the alleged facts.

Our observer may be surprised to find that magistrates do not often send people to prison. Even when they do, it will not be for longer than six months (This is the upper limit of their sentencing powers, though our observer will need to be told that).

Community sentences – for instance, unpaid work or being placed under the supervision of a probation officer – are more frequent. Even where the offence is such that one of these weightier dispositions is available, a fine is very likely. With lesser offences a fine may be the only penalty available, and all that has to be settled is the amount. As the collection of fines is of much importance, a half-day out of a week's sittings may be given over to their enforcement. Offenders in default will have received a summons to explain why and the magistrates will probably require them, when they attend, to make payment by instalments, perhaps by deduction from their pay or benefits. The difficulty of collecting fines from those who present themselves as impecunious will strike any observer. In the last resort, the sanction is a term of imprisonment. This can be awarded only for 'wilful refusal' or 'culpable neglect' to pay what has been ordered. It is only rarely that that point is reached.

Not all the business of magistrates is 'criminal', and not all prosecutions are brought and handled by the Crown. There is a civil jurisdiction, the largest element of which concerns council tax. When this has not been paid by the due date, a local authority's first recourse is to seek liability orders from a magistrates' court in respect of all those liable to pay. Those said to have failed to pay what is due will have been given notice of the application, but very few will attend court to oppose it. A liability order is a declaration that the tax has been properly levied and that a respondent is liable to pay it. The grounds on which the court may refuse to make the order are very narrow.

Magistrates also have powers, rarely exercised, in the enforcement of the collection of income tax. They have an appellate role in some matters within the province of local authorities, for instance the granting or withdrawal of street trading licenses. Here, it may be claimed that the authorities have not followed a proper procedure or that their decisions are ill founded.

Railway companies and other transport authorities prosecute passengers said to have avoided payment of their fares. Local authorities prosecute landlords said to be renting out premises declared to be unsafe or otherwise unfit, party-givers who torment their neighbours with loud music and street-traders trading without a license. It also remains possible for anyone – a private individual – to appear as a prosecutor by way of laying an information at a magistrates' court and obtaining a summons. This sometimes happens in the course of disputes between neighbours, usually after the police have declined to be involved.

A well-informed foreigner may make the best observer of all. Suppose someone familiar with the doing of summary justice in his own country goes along with our observer. If he or she comes from the English-speaking world, there will be much that will be recognisable. The procedure for conducting a trial is likely to be broadly familiar. So, to the observer with some legal knowledge, will be the basis in common law. If he comes from the continent of Europe, he will find much less that is familiar, though even the most striking differences will be less than total. Every country must have a process for dealing promptly and briskly with petty crime, and everywhere procedures will have been worked out which cannot differ greatly, if they are not to jar with intuitions of natural justice. He may however be surprised at the degree to which the business of establishing the facts in the course of a trial is left to the representatives of the two sides, to the minimising of the function of probing and questioning which, from his own standpoint, he would have expected to see fall to the magistrates.

What both of these observers will almost certainly question is the arbitrariness – on the face of it – with which the make-up of the tribunal is determined: why, within one courthouse – and within one legal system – should there be one magistrate on the bench in one courtroom and three in another? This difference cannot be related to a difference in the work done, as this can be seen to be of the same kind, and cases will often have been transferred from one to the other courtroom during the course of the day, as the pressure of business made necessary. A defendant who has waited for two hours to appear before Mr S— in Court I may well be told that his case is now to be called on in Court II, the reason being that the item of business on which Mr S— is engaged is taking him longer than expected. The defendant goes into Court II, is called into the dock and finds himself before a bench of three. The reverse process would have been as likely. To anyone unused to the functioning of magistrates' courts, this may be perplexing; to defendants, already perhaps under stress, it may be worse than perplexing.

There are two ways of constituting a magistrates' court in England and Wales. One, the oldest, is with at least two, usually three, justices of the peace. The other, much less common though less uncommon than it was, is with a single stipendiary magistrate, as he or she was styled until quite recently; the current term is district judge. Justices of the peace – JPs – are laypeople, normally with no legal qualifications, sitting in court part-time, perhaps twice or three times a month, and serving without payment. District judges are legally qualified, either as barristers or solicitors. They sit full-time and almost always singly. In both forms of tribunal, there is a clerk sitting close at hand, but only when he or she is sitting with justices of the peace does the clerk have the role of giving advice to them on the law and on legal procedure.

From a continental perspective, this will be surprising. The fact that laypeople, with no formal qualification in the law, can deal with alleged breaches of the criminal law, determine guilt where this is disputed and pass sentences extending to imprisonment will seem so remarkable that someone to whom it comes as new information is likely to be incredulous. What is so surprising is not the bare fact of lay participation, as it is not unusual in continental jurisdictions for lay assessors to sit with professional judges. It is that lay people may sit by themselves, managing the whole process of low-level criminal justice. To someone from the United States, it may be less surprising, as the office of justice of the peace survives as a relic of the pre-revolutionary period in some of the older states. He is however likely to be surprised by the extent of its present-day employment and its persistence. Only those who have grown up with the arrangement will be able to take it for granted. Some of us will have had it explained to us as children. As a boy, I was told what to expect if I appeared before a magistrates' court: if it were in London, I would be dealt with by one unsuccessful barrister; if in Barchester, by three successful tradesmen. My father might have added that in the country districts of the county of Barset I would appear before a bench drawn largely from the local gentry and the professions. Like many such explanations given to the young, this one was badly out of date and even in its time was not quite accurate. The pay of metropolitan stipendiary magistrates in the nineteenth century was never so poor that only the unsuccessful would have taken the job. It would be even less accurate now: JPs now deal with criminal cases in central London, alongside district judges, as for many years they did not. The composition of the bench is socially much more diverse. Nonetheless, my father's account of the process caught and still catches much of the reality. It is not surprising that well-informed observers from outside find it remarkable. How can the co-existence of two forms of tribunal be explained and defended? The oddity is not only that laypeople have a judicial function; what enhances it is that they discharge this function side by side with salaried professionals.

The first question is therefore why, after so long a period, we seem not to have decided which way of doing summary justice is better. Other questions follow. Is lay justice good enough for its persistence to be acceptable? What are its strengths and weaknesses? In so far as it is imperfect, how could it be made more effective? How should lay magistrates be recruited and prepared for their role? What training should they have, if any? Is lay justice so effective, or could it be made so effective, that there should be nothing else? All these questions – and one can think of others – seem obvious ones, and of a kind to make the casual observer, home-grown or from abroad, wonder how the system just described has come about. I give some account of that in this book.

2.

How it Looks from the Bench

In the next few chapters, I write from my own perspective and ground my remarks in my own experience. This approach has its limitations, but I know of no other way of addressing the subject which offers the same immediacy. What I hope to convey is an impression of what it is like to do the job and to have to deal with a whole variety of difficult issues and perplexities, only some of which will have been predictable. If I have succeeded in this, it should be plain to anyone considering applying for appointment to the bench what is involved in this form of public service. I draw largely on the record of my sittings which I kept at the time. There should be no breach of confidence in this, as nearly all of what I deal with is well in the past, and no one will be identifiable. Quotations from the record are dated, as the law and court procedure change and what may have been the case at one point may not have been at another.

I begin with my own initiation. I was sworn in as a justice of the peace early in 1989. I had given up my full-time employment as a civil servant the previous year, and had applied to be considered for appointment around the same time. The immediate prompt to this was the example of a friend. I remember reflecting that she would be well suited to the role of a magistrate, as I took it to be, and that she ought to be appointed, as in due course she was. This led me to think of myself in the role, and to wonder if I would pass muster. I was conscious of looking for something of the sort. My retirement from paid employment had been unusually early. I had left it with a view to re-entering academic life and had done so by the time I was sworn in. My change of occupation had been satisfactory, but I knew that I also needed a social role. Civil servants are sometimes appointed justices, and I had observed that the demands of the magistracy could be made compatible even with full-time work. It seemed to me that they should be compatible with my ill-focused academic intentions.

What service in the magistracy seemed to promise was the combination of intellectual exercise and down-to-earth usefulness. This was appealing, and I also had a strong enough historical sense to fancy myself standing in a distinguished tradition and to appreciate what went with this. I had no wish to be paid and, if payment had been in question, would have wished not to be. Here were mixed motives, broadly disinterested but not altogether so. I take them to be typical of those seeking appointment to the bench at this or any earlier time. I had neither academic nor professional acquaintance with the law, beyond a year or so of reading for the Bar some twenty-five years earlier. In the course of this, I had passed an undemanding examination in criminal law by the time I decided not to proceed further. I had kept up with criminal law to the extent of reading the law reports in the press, and, as a civil servant, I was used to consulting lawyers over the interpretation of statute. In sum, I was a well-informed layman who was no sort of expert. Expertise is not, of course, what is sought in a justice of the peace. In respect both of qualifications and lack of them, I stood squarely in a very long tradition.

I applied and was called to interview. I had been asked to nominate two referees and had given the names of two friends, a circuit judge and a Cambridge don. The form sent to them for completion was elaborate and must have taken them a long time to complete. The thoroughness of this mode of inquiry had impressed me, and my own preparation had been careful. By the time of interview, I had sat in the gallery of a range of magistrates' courts, both those for adults and those for 'juveniles' (which then meant those under seventeen), observing their procedure and noting their verdicts and decisions on sentence, few of which surprised me. I was interviewed by a panel appointed by the local advisory committee (for which, see Chapter Eight below), made up of a stipendiary magistrate, who took the chair, and two long-standing members of the bench to which I was in due course appointed. Much later, one of these became the only magistrate of my acquaintance to be removed from the bench for misconduct.

As I waited to be called in, I was handed an account of some typical offences, of the kind dealt with by magistrates, with details of offence and offender, and told to study it. This was intended to represent a morning's business in court and, when the interview began, served to break the ice. I was asked how I rated each offence in point of seriousness, on a scale of one to ten. What should a bench be seeking to achieve in passing sentence, bearing in mind the gravity or lack of it of each offence, and what it had been told about the offender? Then came the broader question: what, in general, was the object of sentencing? This question had been easy to anticipate and I had pondered it. My answer was that the prime purpose of sentencing was declaratory. I said that I took the sentence of a criminal court to be, in the first place, a form of social denunciation. The penalty or loss or pain imposed by the court was the means by which denunciation found expression. I ventured to float the word 'vindicative' and to distinguish it from the simply 'vindictive'. I was not pressed further, and I sensed that this answer had been acceptable. On other occasions over the next twenty years, when posed, as I sometimes was, with the same question, I often gave a broadly compatible response, quoting Bacon – *Revenge is a kind of wild justice* – with a view to saying that I took justice to be a kind of tamed revenge. The 'taming' was the transmutation of revenge into something less highly excited, which might then be applied consistently and confined to proper limits. This might have been a better reply to my interviewers.

In due course I was informed that the Lord Chancellor had it in mind to appoint me to the magistracy, formally to the Commission of the Peace for Inner London. Soon after this, I was sworn in, undertaking to 'do right to all manner of people after the laws and usages of this realm without fear or favour, affection or ill will'. The language is archaic, but the undertaking is still resonant. There followed a programme of induction, designed to equip the year's batch of new appointments to sit in court and to be tolerably competent from the start. I remember little of this, but I remember from this time my falling briefly under suspicion of theft. So far as I know, this was the first time I had ever been suspected. I had been supplied with a handbook produced by the Lord Chancellor's Department, which dealt with my new duties and which I needed to read. I had it with me one day, along with a newspaper, when I turned into a bookshop for some inconclusive browsing. When I walked out, with the book wrapped in the paper, I was pursued onto the pavement and asked to show what I was carrying. I saw at once that I had aroused a natural suspicion. It was easy to exculpate myself, the book being what it was. But suppose the book had been a novel, perhaps one bought from the same shop on a past visit and not yet started? The incident made it very clear to me how someone in no way dishonest, yet to some degree absent-minded or pre-occupied, might have fallen under suspicion of an offence which, on conviction, would damage his or her character gravely. The risk of wrongful conviction might have been appreciable. Here was an excellent lesson for someone about to start sitting in judgement.

I was now aware which bench I was to join. This was made up of the justices for one of around a dozen petty sessional divisions or PSDs (as they were then still known) within the wider commission area to which I had been appointed. I was eligible to sit anywhere within the commission area and to sign warrants, but would be on the roster of sittings only of one bench, that of the PSD. In 1989 this had about eighty-five justices, who divided the work with five or six stipendiary magistrates. The split of work was roughly fifty-fifty. As this was a relatively small bench, it did not take me very long to gain some acquaintance with my colleagues. This did not come about in the usual leisurely way of getting to know people. A day on the bench brings about a decidedly close connection with two people, unknown to you to start with, which may last for six or seven hours without a break if the three of you take lunch together. This is likely to leave a strong impression of the others' personalities, which has to be taken on board without preparation. There is an enforced intimacy in the way the work of a magistrate has to be done, which may not be easy or welcome, and those with a gift for easy sociability are at an advantage.

In getting to know my new colleagues personally, I was bound also to sort them out as social types – that is, to see them as standing for something. As I gazed around me at our occasional bench meetings, I saw little to surprise me. Women have been eligible for appointment to the bench since 1918. Here is one striking change from the more remote past. In 1989 nearly two thirds of this bench were women, including the bench chairman. More than a few were the wives of barristers. I observed that many were of that last female generation where it was common to do no paid work after marriage, so leaving time and energy for unpaid work in the public service. Here was an important source of recruits, which in 1989 must have been close to drying up. Otherwise, I found the composition of the bench to be not greatly different from the borough commissions of the past. The well-off middle class was well represented. With this qualification, the bench was broadly representative of the population of England and Wales, though much less so of the population close to hand. As for myself, I would have fitted on to an inner-city bench at any time in the past three centuries – or so I fancied.

I lived just outside the divisional area, and when I was appointed knew little of it. In the course of my travel across it, I could see that its population was largely working class and that a high proportion of it was made up of members of ethnic minorities. I found myself sitting two or three days a month, appreciably more than the Lord Chancellor required as a minimum, though no more than was necessary if the lay bench were to do its proper share of the work. In one respect, I did less than many; as I lived outside the division, I was only rarely asked to sign search warrants and other warrants 'out of hours' – that is, when there was no court sitting. Some of my colleagues, I discovered, were called on to do this very often. Two or three days a month of sitting on the bench, sometimes more, was no more than was necessary for a newly appointed justice of the peace to become effective. If I had been required to start my service on the bench by sitting every weekday for a fortnight, I would have learned the job much more quickly.

After my long-anticipated first sitting, I wrote in my diary:

'Wretched weather – snow and drizzle. I was lucky to get a taxi to take me out to - —. 'The list presented to me at 10.30 had four cases. One we dealt with: a Guilty plea to failing to provide a breath specimen [on suspicion of driving 'over the limit'] from a part-time student living on supplementary benefit – £100 to be paid at £5 per week. The second, also before lunch, was frustrated when the defendant was not produced [from custody]

– apparently because of a prison officers' work-to-rule. A crying scandal.

'In consequence we sat around for over an hour until lunch. Thereafter, one case was adjourned at the prosecution's request; the other was frustrated when the defendant failed to appear, telephoning a plea of tonsillitis. We issued a warrant [for arrest] on being told that she'd done this before on dubious grounds.

'So seemed to end our day when a trial was handed to us, seemingly out of the air [on transfer from another court-room]. Another case of refusing to provide a breath specimen. My view, when we went into the retiring room, was that there was a doubt – he'd refused the second blow into the police-station machine – but I was persuaded out of this. Finding — Guilty. Sentence deferred for his licence to be checked.' (1989)

I deal with what I now think of this first sitting in the course of discussing sentencing. At the time, I was encouraged by what now seems to have been an undemanding day's work, and said so in the diary, going on to say that I had been 'a bit startled by the difficulty of equalising workload and keeping justices employed'. I soon ceased to be startled by this apparent difficulty, though not to be annoyed by it. It continued to shock me, as it still does, that defendants remanded in custody were sometimes not produced when they should have been. This is not unusual:

'A man in Pentonville who should have been committed [to the Crown Court] for affray was *not* produced. The excuse: lack of staff to produce him. This is a public scandal which ought to be notorious.' (1992)

It has yet to become notorious. The inefficiencies of the criminal justice system will have struck our supposed observer from the gallery and will strike those newly appointed to the bench especially sharply. Sometimes, however, what seems to be mere inefficiency is something else: it may be inefficient only by a standard that is not the proper standard.

Over the following twenty years I was to sit on the bench around eight hundred times, nearly always in my own magistrates' court, where I sat as one of a bench of three, or sometimes two. Occasionally, along with another lay magistrate, I sat at the Crown Court to hear appeals from the verdicts or sentences (or both) delivered at magistrates' courts, whether by lay benches or by stipendiary magistrates, now called district judges. Here we sat, without a jury, with a circuit judge or recorder in the chair.

I now quote my record of a day spent sitting in my own court, quite early on in my service, chosen out of many such for its typicality. It is, also exemplary , in the sense that the work seems to have been done competently. This is not to say that everything went well:

'On the bench at -------- — ----------. —. Court II list in Court III. Took the chair in the morning, which was gruelling as usual, and as quickly imprecise in memory. Numerous committals [for Crown Court trial]. We imprison a man for two months for driving when disqualified. We refuse bail in the rather difficult case of a man charged with burglary, a heroin addict. Bail has been refused before and the request is now renewed and supported with a surety offer. I might have granted it, but my two colleagues differed – Mrs X and Mrs Y. In one case – possession of cannabis – the defendant fails to appear and we issue a warrant. He appears after lunch, pleading that he's been delayed by the demands of his job – working in some sort of hostel. We fine him £15 for the Bail Act offence and take a plea on the cannabis offence. He pleads Guilty but, when about to be sentenced, comes up with an excuse: he confiscated the substance from one of the inmates of the hostel. This seems to make the Guilty plea ambivalent and we reject it. The prosecutor then asks for a two-week adjournment to review the case. It is not clear, it seems, whether 'possessing' cannabis is an absolute offence or whether *bona fide* confiscation of it, if established, is a defence. Odd that it isn't clear. A prostitute also arrives late with a similar excuse – couldn't find a baby-sitter. These cases are painfully pathetic.

'In the afternoon we reject two applications for a reduction in the period of disqualification from driving, and find a motorist Guilty *in absentia* for driving without due care. Another case – same charge – which would have had seven witnesses has to be adjourned for lack of time, for the second time! A disastrous failure of listing. For the first time that I remember at ------ — ------ — we have one of the fortunate in the dock – a merchant banker (---- (— ---) —) charged with driving over the limit – pleads Guilty – fine, together with one for speeding, and costs - – £800. The unit fine system would have made it more, and one sees the point of that system.' (1994)

A trial for which seven witnesses were required should have had a full day allotted to it. Its further adjournment on this occasion will have meant that for the second time witnesses attended to no purpose. Attendance is legally obligatory only in the rare cases where the court has issued a witness summons, and it will not have been surprising if they were too disillusioned to turn up on the future date to which we adjourned the hearing. A quite likely outcome will have been the prosecution's dropping of the case. I seem not to have reflected at the time on whose fault all this was. Later on, I would have been inclined to blame the previous bench or stipendiary magistrate for not ensuring that a full day was set aside. Had there been any probing of the need for as many as seven witnesses? Some blame may also have lain with the court's listing-office, which indeed does not have an easy job. Listing cases in a way that keeps every court busy, yet no more than busy, cannot be easy when so much of what happens is unpredictable. If we made a fuss about this fiasco, I did not record it. I am now in no doubt that we should have done.

Apart from this, my record of the day suggests that I would have walked away at the end of proceedings with some satisfaction. Our task had been quite demanding and it seems to have been discharged with competence. It should be said now and with some emphasis, as much of what follows will be concerned with things going badly, that this was in no way unusual. How far our decisions were right – that is, 'right' on some absolute standard – it is of course impossible to know. This makes the judicial function unlike any other.

3.

Sentencing in Principle

First Principles

Passing sentence on those who have pleaded Guilty or been found Guilty is the most conspicuous function of a magistrates' court, indeed of any criminal court. Crown Court sentences are often well publicised and sometimes vigorously criticised, most commonly for being insufficiently severe. Crown Court judges have to acquire some thickness of skin. Magistrates are usually spared the blast to which judges are exposed, though they will not be spared their own belated doubts over decisions for which they shared responsibility, as it is inevitable that some of these will come to seem dubious. Here is part of the pain of the job.

Summary justice is conducted briskly and with only the lightest reference to first principles. For my own part, I found that some reflection on fundamentals was inescapable if I was to be comfortable in what I was doing and consistent in practice. Something of the sort must have been true of many of my colleagues. There was however a convention of reticence, and I must have been typical in seeing little profit in exposing my own position on points of principle. For all that, I picked up enough to realise that there was much diversity of view. This was unsurprising. There is no moral consensus in society on the proper objects of sentencing, nor is there any in the magistracy. The magistracy is representative in this respect, even if – as is often urged – it is insufficiently so in others.

I had made my own position plain enough at my interview. This position, of the kind called retributivist, is often misrepresented, and it is therefore worth saying what it does *not* entail. It does not make severity obligatory, and it is perfectly compatible with leniency. To hold that punishment is the prime object is not to hold that it must always be draconian. Moderation in its exercise may often be judged sufficient, and there will be occasions when a court may well conclude that an offender has been punished enough by a bare appearance in court and exposure of what he or she has done. Fortunately a sentencing court is empowered to deal with such cases with a discharge – that is, a conclusion without penalty – which is usually conditional on not offending again within a specified period, but which may be absolute. I was often to be one of a bench that ended matters with a discharge.

Even where there has to be an immediate penalty, and especially where this is custodial, putting punishment first does not rule out other relevant and useful purposes. The point is simply that these are secondary. In particular, if the offender is committed to prison, this will be *as* punishment and not *for* punishment. The distinction has perhaps become hackneyed, but it is sound and deserves emphasis. There is everything to be said for a constructive employment of every prisoner's time, and it is properly notorious that this is far less often achieved than it should be. The responsibility for this national failure does not lie with the courts.

Many of those with whom I sat on the bench took a view which differed from mine, and I could not be unaware of this difference. I often heard a colleague declare that it was only the reformation of the offender – or at least its prospect – which justified penal measures. This was often expressed as an objection to our passing a custodial sentence, along the lines of 'that won't do him any good'. The principled response to this – which it was tempting to put, though I rarely did – was that the notion of justice is so deeply connected with those of culpability, desert and aptness for punishment that justice cannot be done without those other notions being brought into the frame. Interference with someone's liberty, or even just with his pocket, is justifiable only on the basis that he deserves to be so treated. Desert entails aptness for punishment. Without a well-founded judgment of desert, there is no justification for tampering with the object of concern – the so-called offender.

It is often claimed that deterrence should be the prime object of sentencing. This view was one with which I was uncomfortable, principally because deterrent-sentencing will often amount to passing stiff sentences, not so much on the merits of the offence or of the offender, but to discourage others from offending. The case for doing this is most often pressed where an offence has been especially prevalent or where there has been a sudden surge in the incidence of offending. The nation-wide rioting of August 2011 is a notorious instance. There is ample judicial authority for deterrent-sentencing in such circumstances and both Crown Court judges and magistrates seem to have conformed their sentences to it. The grounds for their doing so were plainly strong. To my own mind, the objection to doing so was stronger, as upping a sentence to discourage others amounts to treating the offender instrumentally – that is, as a means. Is that how a human being should be treated? That it would be as a means to a desirable end hardly meets the objection. To treat the offender as morally responsible is to take him or her to be apt to be dealt with accordingly. To treat him or her, not accordingly, but more severely than that, with the sole object of deterring others, seems wrong in principle – or so I would have argued.

In practice, the gap between an emphasis on retribution and one on deterrence is often minimal. Where that was so, I was not uncomfortable. Suppose that a man is sent to prison by the Crown Court for robbery for a period of some years. The pronouncement of this sentence may be the denunciation of robbery of which the specification of the proper period is the 'language', or it may be a decision of public authority intended to discourage others from robbing. The two versions are easily distinguishable in this way, and the distinction of principle is important, but it may count for little in practice and public opinion disregards it. Sober public opinion calls for deterrence; excited public opinion wants punishment. The means by which these objects should be realised are likely to be broadly the same.

In June 2011, a woman was sentenced to eight months imprisonment for contempt of court. She had been a juror, and had used the internet to communicate with a defendant. The Lord Chief Justice, who presided, is reported to have declared:

'Her conduct in visiting the internet repeatedly was directly contrary to her oath as a juror, and her contact with the acquitted defendant, as well as her repeated searches on the internet, constituted flagrant breaches of orders made by the judge for the conduct of the trial.'

Here the need for the vindication of principle by way of punishment was manifest. The Lord Chief Justice went on:

'If jurors were to be allowed to make their own inquiries about trials they were involved with, the jury system as we know it, so precious to the administration of criminal justice in this country, will be seriously undermined.'

Here it is the need to deter others which was prominent. The two requirements fitted together, as is often the case.

There were times, however, when my moral discomfort persisted. I sometimes had to grant that there were occasions where the need for deterrent-sentencing seemed compelling. To take one example, it is a course the courts are often urged to follow in dealing with those caught carrying knives. I found myself dealing with such cases from time to time, and found them especially difficult when the offender had no significant criminal record to aggravate the bare offence of carrying. Occasionally, one found oneself dealing with a weedy youth with no relevant 'previous', who pleaded that he often felt intimidated and had been carrying a knife for his own protection. This often seemed all too plausible to anyone familiar with the conditions of life in the locality. It was of course no defence in law and could not be allowed to count for much – or anything – if the deterrence of others from carrying knives was to be the over-riding intention. Here I had to live with feeling baffled.

The Basis in Statute

The Criminal Justice Act of 2003 spells out (section 142 (1)) the purposes of sentencing that 'any court dealing with an offender … must have regard to' in reaching its decision. These purposes are stated to be:

> punishment,
> the reduction of crime,
> the reform and rehabilitation of offenders,
> protecting the public,
> and reparation.

So far as I know, this is the first listing-off of such objectives to be found in statute. One wonders what prompted it. Should it be seen as a first step towards establishing criminal justice on a principled and coherent basis? It seems to add too little to be very much of a step. Most magistrates and judges would have said that they had always had regard, in determining sentences, to the purposes now set out.

There is one apparent omission from the list. Incapacitation is not stated as a purpose, unless it is taken to be covered by 'protecting the public'. Those who are given to breaking the law cannot break it when they are in prison. The last twenty years or so have seen both a large increase in the prison population and a significant drop in crime. It would be simplistic to see a plain cause-and-effect relationship here – the matter is too complex for that – but it must be unlikely that there is no such connection, whatever weight is given to it.

The problem with the list is not so much with its make-up as with its application. How should a judge or magistrate understand the relation to each other of the specified purposes? Is just one of them the prime object of sentencing, with the others being left to be accommodated to it? Or are all five purposes of equal importance in principle, the relative weight to be given to each varying with the offence and the offender? This was the point of doubt with which I have been concerned here. I found the latter view to be dominant on the bench to which I was appointed, and I could not escape adapting myself to it.

The sentencing function has always been constrained by parliamentary statute and it became rather more tightly constrained in my twenty years on the bench. Here is the prime control. The Criminal Justice Act of 1991, enacted soon after my appointment, represented a widening of the scope of this control, or so it seemed to those whose determinations were governed by it. One intention behind the Act was clearly to bring a proper uniformity to the courts' use of custodial and community penalties – 'community' denoting such dispositions as probation and unpaid work, or 'community service' as it was then styled. The Act made seriousness the criterion for sentencing across the whole range: a court should not award a community penalty unless it was satisfied that the offence was 'serious enough' for it to be proper, nor a custodial sentence unless the offence was 'so serious' that nothing else would do. The rationale from which these discriminations were derived was obvious, and the drawing of the lines was, so far as I could make out, little different from established practice, at least on the bench where I served. In retrospect, the specifications of the Act can be seen as a long step towards the formation of a national policy for dealing with offenders.

Statute specifies what sentences may be passed by a court in respect of each criminal offence. This may be by way of specifying a maximum, so giving the court adequate powers to deal with what it takes to be the worst instances of offending. In practice, the penalty imposed by the court, of whatever kind, will nearly always be below that maximum, usually considerably below. There are many offences attracting a maximum fine of £1,000, where the fine imposed for the typical offence, at least in the less prosperous parts of the country, might be fifty or a hundred pounds. This does not hold back enforcement authorities, such as TV Licensing, from making heavy play with the maximum figure in publicity designed to discourage breaches of the law. There is a large strain of bluff in such publicity.

Sometimes, though rarely, a minimum penalty will also be specified. There is an instance of this in the sentencing prescribed for the common offence of driving a car while 'over the limit'.

Here the court has to disqualify the offender from driving for a minimum period of twelve months, unless it finds 'special reasons' for not doing so. 'Special reasons' is a term of art, which has been defined with much subtlety by the higher courts. Magistrates may find 'special reasons' in precisely defined cases, which will be infrequent, but that is all they can do: they cannot let themselves off disqualifying offenders because they are aware of the inconvenience, however gross, which disqualification will bring on them, and because they feel sorry for them, as they well may. Driving 'over the limit' will also attract a custodial or financial penalty, as well as disqualification. Which of these it is, and how heavily custodial or financial, will depend on the facts of the case or of the offender. Here the court has its usual discretion, and offenders who are well over the limit often get sent to prison.

Sometimes, in dealing with 'over the limit' cases, I was troubled by the need to depart, as it seemed to me, from principle, the principle being that no one should suffer a penalty except for what he or she had consciously done or failed to do. This seems to matter little in dealing with matters of small importance, where people may be held liable for inactions attributable to lapses of memory. It does not, for instance, seem wrong in principle to fine someone for forgetting to buy a television licence. People should so organise themselves to remember to do such things. Nonetheless, the principle seems to have enough intuitive weight to stand in the way of punishing someone for something more serious, where the penalty would be heavier. Here was the difficulty. To obtain a conviction in cases of driving 'over the limit', it does not need to be shown that there was bad driving. Suppose that a motorist is involved in an accident which was in no way his fault. He may have parked his car in a proper way and another motorist then crashed into it. If the police were then called, he might be breathalysed, as being in a sense a party to the accident, and would have to be disqualified if the reading were high enough. There would be no need to show that his driving of the car before it was parked was below a proper standard. Yet such a driver could be – indeed, would have to be – put off the road for at least twelve months. He would attract this penalty, not because he had been driving badly but because he had been found to belong to a class defined by the *likelihood* of its members driving badly. To proceed on that basis made me uncomfortable. I was however often obliged to do so.

Often the sentencing limits for an offence will be determined simply by the making of an offence summary. This is to say that it has to be dealt with by magistrates, and will be dealt with within their normal sentencing powers. These are expressed in terms of maxima: six months in custody and, for most of my time on the bench, a fine of £5,000. Limits are also specified for community penalties such as unpaid work. This sentence was available throughout my time, though under different designations, with an upper limit of 240 hours and a lower one of 40. It goes without saying that the extent of their powers is the first thing of which a sentencing bench should be aware. Sometimes, though rarely, a bench will return from retirement and announce a sentence, only to be told – as it would have to be – that its sentence is outside what the law permits. Usually this mistake results from the magistrates' failure to turn up the relevant piece of paper or to check what they have determined with their clerk. Very occasionally it will be on account of real doubt. Sentencing powers may be open to argument, and judges too need sometimes to be put right, some time afterwards, by the Court of Appeal.

Guidelines

Magistrates and judges also receive guidance on the exercise of their sentencing powers which lacks the absolute authority of statute but which is still effectively binding. Magistrates have always been obliged to follow the general guidance of the higher courts, in particular that of the Court of Appeal, and this guidance has extended to sentencing. This obligation derives from the fact that the criminal courts compose a hierarchy or structure of command. Magistrates' courts compose the 'lowest', or the basic or busiest level of this structure and work under the general direction of those at the levels above. Failure to do so, or frank refusal, has to be unacceptable, as it would amount to a subversion of the principles on which the criminal courts are founded. Sentences passed on some such pig-headed basis would not however be inoperative, always assuming that they were within the limits laid down by the relevant statute.

At the time of my appointment to the bench, we had recourse to the guidelines supplied by The Magistrates' Association, the quasi-professional body which most of us chose to join. These were applicable to the whole country. They were supplemented by guidelines prepared by the bench itself – that is, by its elected officers in consultation with the senior clerks and the stipendiary magistrates with whom we sat. These were broadly consistent with the Association's guidelines, but had been adapted to take account of local conditions, especially the relative impoverishment none of us could fail to notice. We were counselled not to take our guidelines to amount to a tariff, to be applied in such a way as to cut out private judgement, though my early observation was that they were more likely to be ignored than followed pedantically.

The range of the criminal law is very wide indeed, and both sets of guidelines were limited to dealing with only the most frequent and more serious of the offences which came before us. In respect of each offence and supposing the typical offender, there was an indication of the appropriate penalty or of the range within which such a penalty might fall. The rough-and-readiness of this hardly needs to be spelled out, though I was to find both sets of guidelines helpful rather than not. My colleagues and I were at least better placed than we would have been if we had had nothing but judgements of the Court of Appeal, and perhaps the House of Lords, to rely on. These are always judgements in a particular case, or set of cases, which may well have been somewhat removed from the typical case, which one needed to have in mind if one were seeking *general* guidance.

The availability of The Magistrates' Association's guidelines must have done something at least to correct the inconsistency across benches for which the magistracy had often been criticised. In 1999, the Lord Chancellor, then Lord Irvine, declared that:

> '... society can be hard in its judgment on what it perceives as inconsistency. The public, and the media, look critically at the decisions of bench against bench. They can interpret differences as proof that the magistrates are uncertain among themselves, and that [the] nature of [the] justice you get depends on where you live... That is what makes the sentencing guidelines produced by The Magistrates' Association so important. They are guidelines – they do not curtail your independent discretion to impose the sentences you think are right, case by case... they help to assist the magistracy, to maintain an overall consistency of approach. ... I urge you to follow the guidelines, which are drawn up for your benefit and the benefit of the magistracy as a whole.'

The concern expressed here for the public view of magistrates' decisions is notable, though not perhaps surprising. Ministers have to be sensitive to how the public perceives things. In this field it is as well that they should be, for in a democracy the criminal justice system has to enjoy broad public support if it is to be workable. It may be that in bidding for this support the

Lord Chancellor left his listeners somewhat bemused. If the guidelines then available were to be 'followed', then the discretion to impose the sentences judged to be right would be 'curtailed' – inescapably, for all the easy dismissal of the possibility. It could not be otherwise: curtailment of the eccentric is part of the point of issuing guidance. The problem is that what is likely to appear eccentric may, in the odd unusual case, be what justice requires.

I had been on the bench around ten years when the process for guiding judges and magistrates was developed further. I have referred to the 1991 Criminal Justice Act as a significant first step. The Crime and Disorder Act 1998 established the Sentencing Advisory Panel. This was responsible for research into sentencing and for producing reports and information. The magistracy was not, I suspect, much aware of its proceedings, though the conclusions deriving from them probably lay behind some of the information and briefing supplied to us. A change which bore on magistrates directly came with the passage of the Criminal Justice Act 2003. This re-enacted, in somewhat modified terms, the 'seriousness' specifications of the 1991 Act and perpetuated the Sentencing Advisory Panel. A larger innovation was its creation of a new body, the Sentencing Guidelines Council, with a role that was implicit in its title.

The Council issued guidelines, either of its own volition or by way of proposals from the Sentencing Advisory Panel or from the Home Secretary. It so doing, it had to take into account the need for consistency, the cost and relative effectiveness of different sentences in preventing offending, and the need to promote public confidence. These guidelines were either indications of an appropriate range of penalty for serious and frequent offences or guidance of a more general character, which extended to such topics as the credit to be accorded those who pleaded Guilty and domestic violence. In this respect, the Council continued, more systematically and with the support of the Panel, what was already being done.

The Council also set out more precisely the process to be followed by those passing sentence in discharging their role. This was not so much an original prescription as a substantial formalisation of the process of decision-making. For some time, this had been impressed on new recruits to the bench and reinforced by the regular training offered to all. A template was offered and the members of a bench in their retiring-room and judges sitting solo were expected or, more precisely, obliged, to work their way through it. They were required to appraise in a systematic way the harm done by the offender and his or her culpability, and then to consider what there was about the offender which might mitigate the offence and so tend to a lessening of penalty. In announcing the sentence reached in this way, the court was required to give its reasons, in particular explaining why it had done so when, for some good reason, it had departed from the relevant guideline.

The effect on the lay magistracy of this formalisation of procedure was, in my experience, appreciable. It may be seen as a step in the steady reshaping and direction of the office of Justice of the Peace. This aspect, unsurprisingly, attracted little public attention. Other aspects might well have attracted more notice. One was a provision of the Act which might have seemed to be at least the germ of direct control over sentencing by ministers. It was for the Home Secretary to make proposals on sentencing to the Council. On this provision, one commentator observed: 'The Sentencing Guidelines Council must consider such proposals… and, in effect, whether or not to act upon them. This discretion represents a critical buffer in terms of preserving the independence of the judiciary'. One might add: '… and also of the magistracy'.

Is there a point of principle here? The commentator just quoted, the editor of the Waterside Press guide to the 2003 Act, clearly thinks there is, though he seems to find the 'buffer' firm enough to prevent the principle being breached. I agree in both respects, and can see no grounds for supposing that the arrangement prescribed in the Act should not have worked satisfactorily. More generally, to regard the independence of judicial agents in discharging their role as vital is not to hold that they should take no account of the foreseeable consequences of their sentencing decisions. To question this seems to come close to suggesting that there is an ideal ignorance which judges and magistrates should seek to achieve and preserve. On the contrary, the more relevant information they have the better, and there are kinds of information which can only come with authority when they come from ministers.

Other kinds of relevant information include that which bears on the state of penal institutions. The number of those in custody rose steadily over my twenty years on the bench. It has become notorious that the prisons are over-crowded and so, in many ways, less effective. How far should magistrates take this into account in deciding whether or not to commit someone to prison? It need not count for very much, but should it count for anything, on those occasions when the arguments for and against a custodial sentence are finely poised? In my earlier days on the bench the majority view was that it should not. I recall colleagues of much experience insisting that we should pass the sentence we judged proper and not try to do the Home Secretary's job for him. I found it difficult to argue against this, which has its basis in a principled view of the limits of a judge's or magistrate's role, but I was relieved when Lord Bingham, then Lord Chief Justice, sitting judicially, declared that over-crowding in prisons was something the courts could properly take into account.

I have spoken of the Sentencing Guidelines Council in the past tense, as it was not long before both the Council and the Panel were replaced. Their successor body, The Sentencing Council, was established by the Coroners and Justice Act of 2009 and became effective, after my retirement from the bench, in 2010. This has been not so much a replacement as a strengthening and amalgamation. The Sentencing Council has a wider remit than that of the two earlier bodies. As well as creating guidelines and monitoring their application, it is required:

'to assess the impact of sentencing practice and non-sentencing related factors, and to promote awareness of sentencing matters; it may also be required to assess the impact of policy and legislation proposals relating to sentencing. In formulating guidelines the Council will consult widely.'

I have quoted from the advertisement issued by the Ministry of Justice in November 2009, inviting applications for membership of the newly created body. Though this is clumsily put – what are 'non-sentencing related factors? – its drift is apparent.

The Sentencing Council has fourteen members, eight 'judicial', including a magistrate, and six others, chosen for their experience within relevant fields. In this, it resembles the Sentencing Guidelines Council. From the point of view of the magistrate or judge directly concerned with sentencing – and perhaps with not much else – the difference between the two bodies which matters most is that it is declared in the 2009 Act that those passing sentence 'must follow' the new Council's guidelines. Previously they were required only to have regard to them and to state their reasons, for the record, when they departed from them. There was much concern in the magistracy when this change of formula came into prospect and some lobbying against it. What has mitigated the concern is the further prescription that a guideline need not be followed when to do so would not be in the interests of justice. In such an instance, they can depart from it, stating for the record their reasons for doing so. This seems to offer a let-out of prime importance. Anyone who has had to exercise authority in a way that requires the application of rules will know that to do this quite inflexibly will sometimes have consequences which no one would wish for or be prepared to defend.

The Chairman of the Sentencing Council, then Sir Brian Leveson, a member of the Court of Appeal, showed himself to be well aware of the sensitivity of this point. In an interview with *The Times* (3 June 2010) soon after the Council had begun to function, he referred to what I have called the let-out in saying that 'Guidelines are not tramlines'. He went on to say that he hoped there would be a greater consistency of sentencing across the country. In the same interview he spoke also of the new Council's extended functions, in particular collecting information on sentencing and equipping itself to advise Governments on the impact and cost of proposed legislation. It may be surprising that the Home Office was not already doing much of what is now to be assigned to the Council. Perhaps it was, and successive ministers have been unwilling to listen. In either case, the long-term consequences of the 2009 enactment may therefore be large.

Plea Bargaining

It is sometimes urged that proof should be required in every case, even in those – the great majority – where culpability is not disputed. Those who argue for this are alive to the possibility of admissions of guilt coming from those who do not know the law and who might have had an arguable defence in law. They may also come from defendants who have been persuaded by their own advisors to agree to plead Guilty to a lesser charge on condition of a more serious one being dropped. Sometimes, it is argued, the defendant would like to deny the lesser charge too but has concluded that the risk in doing so would be too great. This, it is argued, is a perversion of justice, in that Guilty pleas – which will not be probed – may come from persons in no way culpable. Guilty pleas should therefore not be accepted. Whatever the defendant says or does not say, the prosecution case should have to be proved.

There is an obvious counter-argument to this, which is that such a change to criminal procedure would greatly increase both the cost of prosecuting offences and the amount of court-time required to deal with them. The appreciable cost to public funds would seem, to most people, to serve little purpose. It would also require magistrates – and juries – to give much of their time to listening to proof of facts which no one would be concerned to deny to be facts. That would not make the job appealing to potential recruits. This practical objection, strong as it is, is hardly a rebuttal. It is an asertion on the other side, carrying much weight.

Considerations of this kind bring up the whole large question of 'plea bargaining' All experienced magistrates will have registered the occasional employment of something like it. They may come into court to deal with a charge which, on their scale, is serious – say, one of assault occasioning actual bodily harm (ABH). They are then asked to permit the withdrawal of this charge and the substitution of one less serious – say, common assault – to which the defendant would plead Guilty. Where the defendant was legally represented, this seemed unobjectionable – at least, I never raised an objection, nor do I recall ever sitting with a colleague who did. Reflecting on the point now, I have to admit that when we then proceeded to deal with the offender (as he or she would at that stage be referred to), we may well have been sentencing him for something which he would have denied altogether, if he had been left to himself.

Wherever pleas of Guilty are permitted, there will be an opening for plea bargaining. Indeed, the option of pleading Guilty is in itself close to being an offer of an abated sentence. Such abatement is standard and hardly controversial (30% off a custodial sentence is common where there has been a prompt admission of guilt). What may make talk of plea bargaining alarming is awareness of what happens elsewhere. This may come from accounts in the press of its employment in the United States, where it has the form, at least in those accounts, of plain intimidation. I cannot discuss those here, though I grant that, at least as reported, what sometimes happens is chilling. From the accounts to be found in the press, a defendant who persisted in denying the charge put to him – when that charge was at all serious – would face the ruinous costs of mounting a defence, over a period in which he might be in custody. He would also face the prospect of a custodial sentence, on conviction, of extraordinary length. Such reports as these have made a strong and widespread impression.

There is nothing quite like that – at least at present – in England and Wales. A recent change may however seem not entirely different. The cost of criminal proceedings and the need to control and minimise it has very recently prompted the introduction of a Criminal Courts Charge. This has received much attention, and steady criticism – on at least one occasion, in September 2015, from a Crown Court judge who declared how much he disliked having to impose it. In brief, this is a charge levied on those found Guilty, much more heavily than on those who pleaded Guilty, as they will have brought about the expence of a trial. This surely means that there will now be a further incentive to plead Guilty

– on top of the standard abatement for Guilty pleas – which may distort the doing of justice.

Plea bargaining deserves separate treatment, especially if the element of bargaining is extended to the tribunal; for instance, the judge, or a bench of magistrates, is invited to promise a lenient disposition – for instance, ruling out a custodial sentence – in return for a Guilty plea. We are as yet nowhere near that possibility. I refer to it here, only by way of saying that it would complicate the magistrates' role appreciably. It is only because that role is comparatively simple that its discharge, in large part by lay people, is feasible. I return to this point below.

Fines

The power to impose fines is a main component of the armoury available to courts of summary jurisdiction. It is much the most frequent penalty imposed by magistrates' courts and may be the only one available, as the statute creating an offence will often make it punishable only by that means. Many a day in court is spent imposing fines on offenders, often numerous, which will be handed out at speed, there being no question, or even possibility, of anything else. It therefore matters that, in one obvious and important respect, a financial penalty differs from both imprisonment and a community penalty, such as unpaid work. This is that the forfeiture of a given sum of money will affect people to very different degrees. A fine of a few hundred pounds will be a decidedly severe penalty for many offenders and one which they will find it hard to accommodate, especially when the sentence is unexpected. The same sum may be little more than trivial for the well-off, being no more than the cost of a boozy lunch with friends. This will strike most people as unfair.

This inequality of pain is not peculiar to financial penalties: it applies to some degree to custodial and community penalties. A sentence of three months imprisonment may be an appalling shock or merely a disagreeable interlude. Offenders and all their circumstances differ greatly. Men who have been to boarding schools are said to have a head-start in adapting to a first spell in prison, a distinction, if it is that, which can hardly be taken into account in deciding whether or not to send a man to prison and, if so, for how long. To complain about the uneven bearing on offenders of custodial and community penalties is to invite the response 'too bad'. Such a response may be merited there, but it hardly serves in the case of financial penalties, which seem to present a *special* problem to anyone concerned for equality of treatment and for the avoidance of even the appearance of class-bias in the judicial system.

Magistrates have always been exhorted to take account of the offender's means in calculating fines and, in my own experience, have always tried in a rough and ready way to do so. It must have seemed obvious that they needed to do so systematically. In the early 1990s came the introduction of what were termed 'unit fines'. This was a procedure by which the sentencing court imposed a number of 'units' by way of penalty, a cash value being put on the unit once the offender's means had been ascertained or calculated. All magistrates went through a process of familiarisation with this procedure. They had not been using it for very long before it was wound up with little ceremony, the Home Secretary of the day (Kenneth Clarke) declaring simply and breezily that it had been found not to work. We therefore went back to doing what we had done before. While the object of a rough equivalence of deprivation was unchanged, the more systematic approach was aborted.

I need say little about the causes of this fiasco, as the innovation is now history. The history of botched projects is rarely of any interest. What I recall is that benches were left to decide for themselves what to do in cases where the offender, convicted in his absence, had told the court nothing about his means. As they had differed widely over the course to take, there had been much critical, and sometimes derisive, comment in the press on the range of outcomes. This was a main reason, but there may have been others, for the general apprehension that the details of the scheme had been badly worked out. It still seems odd that it was wound up so quickly, instead of being amended.

A second attempt at realising the same object came fifteen years later. The Sentencing Guidelines Council provided judges and magistrates with a grid to be used for the working out of fines. Employment of the grid brings together a judgment on the seriousness of the offence and a calculation of the offender's disposable income. There was less scope here for the process to go wrong than there had been with unit fines. The operation of the procedure, while it slows down the business of sentencing, does so for a good reason, that of enforcing closer attention to the facts. This procedure, or something of the sort, is now in use and seems set to become permanent. It must be admitted that it represents no more than a large step towards equality of deprivation, and not its achievement. A fine would have to be very large if it were to penalise the decidedly rich offender to the same degree as the offender living on benefits. If it were very large, however, it would in all likelihood seem disproportionate to the offence, as the offence might be trivial. The disproportion would then violate another principle of sentencing, that of the proper correspondence of offence and penalty. It was the – very occasional – imposition of fines of a thousand pounds or so for such offences as dropping a negligible quantity of litter which discredited the unit fines experiment.

One benefit which the present procedure should bring is that fines set at a proper level at the start – so that they are not excessive – should be easier to collect. Fairness to the impecunious offender and feasibility of collection are most likely to be achieved together. However, difficulties remain. A defendant – that is, someone not yet convicted – is obliged to supply the court with information as to his means. What should the court do if, for whatever reason, there is no declaration? It is possible to adjourn the hearing to another date and to require the defendant's attendance, if the problem is that he is absent. This will delay the winding-up of what may be a trivial matter and, if done on a large scale, will increase the workload of the court and of its supporting staff.

What are the declarations of means which magistrates should have before them worth in practice? It would be rash to assume that those who supply information about their means will do so fully. The offences for which fines are imposed may well be offences of dishonesty. In those cases the court will be asking someone who has been found to be dishonest, or who has admitted it, to state facts which, if honestly stated, will be to his disadvantage. What should we expect in such a case? It is hard to estimate the scale of this problem. Many offenders, notably (I fancy) many convicted of motoring offences, will be people who are scrupulous in all their financial affairs. Someone who makes a complete return of income to the tax authorities is likely to be equally candid here. There are many such, but also – everyone knows – many others who act differently. It is of course an offence to make a false declaration, and the general awareness of this probably leads many offenders to tell the truth. There is however next to nothing, to the best of my observation, by way of enforcement. I cannot recall a single instance of a prosecution for failure to provide a statement of means or for making an incomplete or deceptive statement. There must have been such, but they must have been very infrequent.

The coercive force of regular successful prosecution seems to be quite lacking.

As for the difficulty of collecting fines, there has been no comparable fresh initiative, but there has been steady pressure on those operating the collection system, including magistrates, to be more efficient. Justices will quite often spend a day in court on nothing other than fine-enforcement. Those who appear before them will in all likelihood have been given 'time to pay' by the court that imposed the sentence. This means that offenders are allowed to pay in instalments, over a period. If not, such an arrangement can be set up. The court is able to order deductions from pay and from welfare benefits. Coercive measures, such as the seizure of goods by bailiffs may be ordered if others are ineffective. Finally, if all else fails, committal to prison is an option, though only by way of last resort. To put it simply, the court cannot send someone to prison for not having the money or the goods needed to pay a fine, but it may do so if it is satisfied that he is able to pay and chooses not to. In consequence, imprisonment for non-payment is now rare. As the prisons are so grossly over-crowded, this is hard to regret, though magistrates quite often suffer from a sense of impotence at the end of a day spent on fine-enforcement.

Some criminal justice systems closely comparable to ours do not make much use of fines. This may come as a surprise to anyone, such as myself, who has been conditioned by experience to take the fine to be the basic penalty available to courts of summary jurisdiction and to be one which is bound to be used often. In the early 1990s, I joined in a magistrates' visit to Chicago with a view to observing how things were done within a legal tradition with its roots in English common law and so closely comparable to our own. I was surprised to learn that the power to impose fines was little used. The question of matching fines to offenders' means therefore hardly came up. I was told that the main reason for not imposing them was the difficulty of collection: it was very easy for offenders to avoid payment simply by slipping across the state border. In consequence, what we term community sentences were used a lot. The variety of these and the scope available to the sentencing judge were both remarkable. Beyond this, no reminder was needed of the frequency of recourse to custody in the USA. We should not be too quick to conclude that there is no alternative to the heavy use of financial penalties.

4.

Sentencing in Practice

Not a few offenders are effectively outside the range of punishment. In September 2012, after I had left the bench, I read a press report of a sentence passed by a district judge on a homeless man who had admitted stealing a ready-mixed vodka and tonic drink from Marks & Spencer. He told the judge that he stole the drink in order to be sent to prison, so as to get a roof over his head. The value of the drink was £2.15. The judge refused to send him to prison, no doubt on the grounds that the offence was not 'so serious' that this was justifiable. Ruling out custody on the facts before him was certainly in line with the intention of Parliament that 'petty' offenders should be kept out of prison. So what was the judge to do with the man before him, who had been given a conditional discharge for a similar petty theft only the previous month. He now fell to be sentenced for that earlier offence, as well as the present one, having broken the condition of the discharge. A further conditional discharge would have been absurd. What the judge did was fine the offender £50 for the first offence and £100 for the second. According to the press report, he accepted that the offender had no money. We were not told how he addressed that difficulty, but probably he tried to arrange for the fines to be paid by way of deduction from social security benefits.

Such very petty, and very frequent, offences do not often get the attention of the press. The case reported was rightly thought to be of general interest on account of the stubbornness of the problem it throws up. What course would I have pressed on my colleagues, if we had had to sentence on those facts? In all likelihood, I would have fallen back on that which the district judge adopted. I would however have been tempted to declare that the offence, taken with the earlier one, was 'so serious' that custody was an option, pointing to the speed of its repetition and to the need to deter persistent shoplifters. I would have done this with a straight face (so far as I could manage that), and then imposed a sentence of ten days or so. That would not even have met the offender's wish for a comfortable berth for the winter, but it would have had a proper declaratory value and would have spared an overloaded system the further burden of collecting tiny sums by way of fine. Such a course would have smacked of sophistry, but the discomfort attending on that might have been easier to bear than the consciousness of doing something futile.

As it was, it must have been likely that the offender would have left court feeling he had got away with it. The penalty was a financial penalty, and he had no money. He might also have felt that his next offence would have to be much more serious to produce the desired outcome, a waterproof roof over his head. Assault on a police officer has its own satisfaction for some people and it very often leads to custody. It might have seemed to be just what was needed. That would have been an unhappy outcome.

There are certainly grounds for holding short custodial sentences to be generally undesirable, leaving aside the somewhat artificial criterion of 'seriousness'. This point is often made. As short sentences, up to six months, are all that magistrates' courts can pass, it is arguable that magistrates' and district judges' powers should be restricted so as to remove the option of custody. I have not indeed heard it argued, but I recall the occasion on which an assembly or association of prison governors called for the option to be confined to district judges. This proposal can hardly have been thought through, as it would certainly be unworkable in practice. District judges and lay benches often sit side by side, with cases being transferred between them throughout the day, so as to even-out the workload and to ensure that, if possible, everything is disposed of by the end of the day. If the sentencing powers of the two ceased to be the same, liability to be sent into custody would become a matter of chance. It is unsurprising therefore that, so far as I know, this suggestion has not been repeated. The wider criticism of the passing of short sentences has however continued. In 2006, in the course of recording a day in court, I noted:

'*The Times* today [11 May] carried a report of some declaration from the Lord Chief Justice, addressing some body in Oxford: avoid custody, especially short sentences, as these are ineffective for rehabilitation of damaged characters and social pests (likely to be one and the same) ... Upstairs, at lunchtime, I mentioned the LCJ's pronouncements to three district judges having their meal: the reaction was along the lines of 'he ought to come and sit here', meaning how else do you deal adequately with such cases [as those we had, separately, been dealing with over the morning]?' (2006)

My own first reaction to what the Lord Chief Justice had said had been one of agreement. It is entirely plausible to claim that efforts at the rehabilitation of a homeless man, quite probably, but not certainly, someone of the kind he had in mind – 'damaged', social pest' – are impracticable when the spell to be served is only short. My second reaction was that rehabilitation is not the single, and perhaps not even the prime object of imprisonment. It was on grounds such as that which, I imagine, my district judge colleagues' reaction was based.

By chance, I had spent that morning as one of a bench which had had to take two sentencing decisions which brought these points sharply to mind:

> 'One [offender] had pleaded Guilty to driving while disqualified and being over-the-limit: third offence of the latter, second of the former. Community penalties had been tried before, most recently last December. The drink level was 102 – that is, he was very drunk... The other was a Portuguese man pleading Guilty to ABH [Actual Bodily Harm] – assault on his girlfriend, at home and in the presence of children. Here I think rehabilitation might have been tried, but how would the turpitude of what he did have been recognised and denounced? So we gave him four months – very little in the light of the Crown Court maximum of five years. We gave the motorist three months – also lenient, I think.'

My passing reference to rehabilitation now seems facile; I probably had in mind the anger-management course which is one of the means by which probation officers address conduct of the kind that this offender had evidenced. Such a disposal would have had something to be said for it. The choice was between that and the frankly punitive sentence which we passed, trusting, I have no doubt, that it would also have a deterrent effect, not only on the present offender but on others. Here was a line of conduct – 'at home and in the presence of children' – where deterrence had to be a prime consideration. With this case fresh in my mind, my district judge colleagues' reaction must have been quite unsurprising.

Writing some years later, I continue to be surprised at the near-unanimity of pronouncements from senior judges, ministers of the Crown and academic experts to the effect that short custodial sentences achieve little, clog up the gaols, cost too much – and so on. I am surprised, because it is surely very likely that even a short spell in prison must deliver a dreadful shock, at least for a first offender, and more especially for someone no longer young. It is no doubt true that there will be insufficient time for remedial work, but there must be many cases where this will not be worth attempting. Often the offence will have been frankly opportunist; the offender did something because he or she expected to get away with it: the purse or handbag – 'was there'. Why not chance it? Other such examples are drivers 'over-the-limit', drivers disqualified from driving, and often (not always) assailants. Here a short shock should be ample punishment, and the public awareness that it is a likely sanction will, on any plausible view, have a significant deterrent effect. An instance of this is the custodial sentence passed in 2013 on Chris Huhne, one-time minister and MP, and on his then wife, for agreeing to lie about which of them had been driving a car.

I gave some account in Chapter Two of the first occasion of my joining with colleagues on the bench to pass sentence. One of those to be sentenced was a part-time student living on supplementary benefit. He had pleaded Guilty to failing to provide a breath specimen, when required to do so by a police officer as part of the process for dealing with drunken drivers, or suspected drivers. The sentence was a fine of £100 to be paid at £5 per week. We would also have disqualified him from driving for a year or more if the refusal came after he had been driving, as it probably did. To the observer in the gallery, such as I had recently been, a fine of £100 might have seemed on the low side, even at the monetary values of 1989. It would not however have been over-lenient in relation to his income, if his income were indeed what he told us. I have no doubt that in fixing the amount I deferred to my two experienced colleagues. This cannot have been a difficult sentencing decision.

None of the other three cases listed came off: we adjourned one at the prosecutor's request; in another the defendant failed to appear and we issued a warrant; in the third the defendant, who was in custody, was not produced as he should have been, on account (it seemed) of a prison officers' work-to-rule – 'a crying scandal,' I recorded. The adjournment may have been quite proper, but the effective collapse of the list was a foretaste of what I was going to have to get used to, and did get used to, but to which I was never resigned. Then, after much hanging around, we took over a trial from an adjoining court, also of a man charged with refusing a specimen. We found him Guilty, after some argument, but sentence was deferred for his driving licence to be checked.

Here was a useful beginning: not too taxing and, in its way, enlightening. Many of the sentencing decisions I will deal with in this chapter were more problematic at the time of making them and of a kind to leave an uncomfortable trace in the mind:

> '... case of 'flashing' man of 25 or so, exposed himself before a girl of ten outside school and started masturbating. Standing in the dock he seemed the image of shame and misery. Fined £200 + homily from the chair that he'd now be on a sexual offenders' register, so he'd better look out. I think this was right, having argued against the alternative of a conditional discharge. There needed to be a penalty but it had to be immediate and limited.' (1990)

I had heard it said by judges and by magistrates of experience that those who commit sexual offences of a graver kind often turn out to have begun that course of conduct with 'flashing'. It was therefore important that we should sentence the man before us aright. The option of a conditional discharge had its appeal with that in mind, as the condition would have been that he committed no further offence for a specified period. That meant that if he were to have done the same thing again he would have been sentenced on that future occasion for this earlier offence as well as that later one. Here, it may be argued, there would be a strong deterrent. I was however moved by the consideration that the offence against the child needed to be registered by an immediate penalty. Hence my objection. For all its deterrent effect, a conditional discharge is likely to seem a 'let-off'.

Here was the basis for an argument that might have been protracted. As it turned out, the three of us seem to have reached a conclusion with little difficulty. All that now strikes me is that we seem not to have considered putting the offender on probation, in the hope that a probation officer would have steered him towards therapeutic help of the kind that would have made future offending less likely. But was such help available? Would a probation order have been an effective way of obtaining it? Looking back over twenty years, I find no reason to suppose we did the wrong thing. I will never know, of course, whether we did or not. It is one of the peculiarities of passing sentence in a court of law, and an unhappy one, that one rarely discovers what happened next. This means that it is hardly possible to learn from one's mistakes, however sure one is that one must be making some mistakes.

I find from the record I kept that, in my early days on the bench, I was generally more in favour of a punitive approach than were my colleagues. I find it hard to say how often I prevailed when we retired to consider what to do, not I think all that often. I was rarely so sure that I was right that I argued very hard:

'... case of a man of fifty-two who'd assaulted his co-habitant quite nastily – drunken row after a party – the woman giving evidence in mitigation on his behalf and now wanting to marry him. We gave him twelve months probation in line with the report, I originally demurring, favouring something tougher. In the same way we gave a conditional discharge for a year to a man who'd assaulted a policeman, not very badly, after being searched for drugs – again I thought not enough.' (1990)

The first of these decisions was of a kind which I never ceased to find perplexing. For many years now there has been an effective lobby for the point that violence against women in a domestic context should be treated as more serious, not less, on account of its context. The home, it was urged, should be a place of security, and its violation should be treated as an aggravation. The attitude of disregard attributed to the police, fairly or not – 'it's only a domestic' – was unacceptable.

This point has been well made, and who would now argue against it? The difficulty for the sentencing-court comes when the female victim, usually the one who has called in the police and started proceedings, regrets doing so and backtracks. It will be unusual for her to appear for the defence, as in the case above, but failure to turn up to testify for the prosecution will generally be enough to abort proceedings. The alleged victim's evidence may indeed be dispensable. It is now quite common for her injuries to be photographed at the scene, and a conviction may be sought on that evidence only. The prosecution is quite within its rights in so proceeding, but I would have been uncomfortable if I had been aware that this was being done against the alleged victim's wishes. Conviction would in all probability damage a relationship with the defendant which the woman, however perversely, might want to maintain. Is that not a matter for her decision?

On the other side, there is the strong point that acts of violence are an offence against the Crown – that is, against the public – so that proceeding with a prosecution is not a matter for the alleged victim only, and very properly not. In the now remote past, it was for the victim to prosecute. The taking over by the Crown of ordinary criminal cases was a decided advance and few people would deny that it is much to the advantage of those who would have found private prosecution impracticable. Hence my perplexity.

I find, re-reading my notes, that I was much exercised in my early days on the bench by this need to see that sentences were punitive to the right degree:

> '... a case of driving while disqualified, driving while drunk, taking and driving away, etc... Dreadful record. As clear a case for custody as can be imagined, yet we argued about it. The grounds for doing otherwise were that he was trying to deal with an addiction and had an appointment for treatment. We gave him three months in total, which I thought lenient: 2-1 split, Mrs X dissenting. The other case was of a woman charged with theft and obtaining property by deception – a drug addict on probation (conditions breached by the offences) who was alleged, with some evidence, to have gone quite a long way to ending the addiction. six-months probation – effectively nothing as she was already on probation.

> I feel unhappy about both cases for opposing reasons: too hard? too soft? *More* unhappy of course about the first, where we had an outburst from the dock after sentence: 'What more can I do?' etc... There's a peril to the soul in all this...' (1991)

My notes are too scanty for it to be possible to form any view on whether what I concurred in over twenty years ago was well founded. It was claimed for the first offender that he was tying to deal with his addiction and that he had an appointment: that is easily asserted and the claim may or may not have been substantiated. The stronger argument for what we did now seems to me to be deterrence, not the retribution which was foremost in my mind; we may have done the right thing, if for the less compelling reason.

My notes of my early days on the bench often record my sense that we were over-lenient. Shortly after the above,

> '...a case of assault (wife-bashing) we dealt with with a conditional discharge and £100 compensation – too lightly in my view – it's hard to get people to take these cases seriously enough – though my colleagues in this case were both women... A case of cruelty to a dog – £50 fine plus heavy veterinary fees and costs – total c. £350 – the wife-basher will pay a total of £125' (1991)

A journalist with an article to write could easily have made something of this. I noted too little of the detail of either case to be able to show that our course of conduct had been reasonable, though I now take it that it pretty certainly was. For one thing, the wife-basher probably had no money and the man convicted of cruelty was more happily placed. What is more, the marriage between the woman-victim and her assailant was very likely still in being – or so we might have been told; taking money from the assailant would only have made things even harder for the couple of which he was one half. How far should the court take account of such considerations?

With experience, I got more assertive:

> '...Mrs P took the chair in the afternoon, when we had a whole list of Department of Social Security prosecutions. Here I think I was of use, arguing the other two into taking a reasonably tough line. We gave three community service orders, two of eighty, one of fifty hours. This was lenient – justifiably so – but not as absurdly inadequate as it would have been if left to them. This

weakness is understandable – the procession of misery through the dock is certainly affecting.' (1997)

What I wrote here might have served as a record of my approach and reactions on any other of the occasions when I had to deal with this list. It was rare to sit with colleagues who were not in broad agreement, but that did happen:

'I took the chair after lunch and presided over the hearing of a string of social security fraud cases. We gave six community service orders. J— [sitting with me] declared his dissatisfaction with our whole line of approach. What he'd have done instead never became clear. The ground of his repugnance was, I think, sympathy with the circumstances of the offenders – all 'black', nearly all women, all poor. I shared this sympathy but, I suppose, didn't let it outweigh my sense that mendacity – the repeated making of false statements – had to be taken seriously and that sentencing had to be deterrent. What to do instead: that's the problem.' (2000)

What we did here was by no means unmerciful: if the sums involved had been substantial, it would not have been unjust to have sent the offenders to prison. To that extent, J— had his way. It could even be said that, for those before us, the sentences which we passed – unpaid work, as it would later come to be called – was less of a punishment than a fine would have been. That line of thought is however somewhat dangerous, as it might lead to the conclusion that for the same offence the well-off could pay large fines while the impecunious could be made to do unpaid work. This would look like – and surely be – the well-off getting away with it.

When I started to sit in the Crown Court, dealing not only with appeals but, at that time, with committals for sentence, I reacted in much the same way:

'I argued unsuccessfully for a short spell of custody but was not unhappy to be voted down: the classic sentencing difficulty – nasty offences which required demonstrative punishment committed by a weak and pathetic, if threatening, person. In such a case the common belief that prison is brutalising, and incompatible with remedial treatment, leads to a determination to avoid its use if at all possible. So thought the judge, and the other justice agreed. Of course the only possible resolution is to change the quality of life in prison: it's soft where it shouldn't be and appalling in ways it's not meant to be'. (1994)

Visits to penal institutions form part of the initial training of justices and continue to be offered. This should ensure against a custodial sentence being passed by someone who has no idea what it amounts to. The awareness derived from a visit will however be no more than superficial: a conducted tour of the landings followed by a chat-session with a senior member of the prison staff. I formed the view of life in prison expressed in the words just quoted from reading the memoirs and reminiscences of discharged prisoners, sometimes in the press, also in book-form. On the rare occasions when a well-educated man of some notoriety (I know of no women) serves and completes a prison term, his writing a book about it often follows quickly; it gives him the last word. The reports of the playboy and journalist 'Taki' (*Nothing To Declare*, 1991) and, at some length, of Jeffrey Archer (*Prison Diary*, three volumes, 2002/03/04) are both impressive, more especially as neither author began with anything like a soft attitude to the treatment of offenders. I was under no illusion that imprisonment was anything other than highly disagreeable.

The obvious alternative to custody is what is now called a community sentence. I touched on this in the previous chapter. This disposition should be considered for those whose offences are 'serious enough' for it to be appropriate, while not being 'so serious' that only custody is adequate. The verbal distinction is to be found in the 1991 Criminal Justice Act and it has been maintained in subsequent enactments. It is convenient, and sentencers are now well used to it. Community sentences come in a variety of forms; the most commonly employed are probably a probation order and what is now called an order with an unpaid work requirement. The second of these was originally called a community service order, then a community punishment order. This change in designation catches, rather nicely, a shift in attitude, at least among legislators, towards the frankly descriptive, and implicitly punitive, and away from the high-minded and euphemistic. The change seems to me for the better, and I wonder if it indicates a trend. If conscription to the armed forces were to be reintroduced, would it be called conscription, rather than National Service?

Community sentences are often employed by magistrates' courts. I was frequently one of a bench which delivered one, much more frequently than when I joined in sending an offender into custody. A difficulty which attends them is that the offender has to co-operate; he continues to be a free agent, which he would not be if he were in prison. In particular, he or she had to turn up punctually for a session of unpaid work or for a meeting with a probation officer, and would sometimes fail to do so, either wilfully or on account of being too disorganised to do what was required of him. Such problem cases might be identified at the time of sentencing or after a community sentence had been passed:

> ' … a twenty-year old who'd pleaded Guilty earlier to taking-and-driving-away. We had a pre-sentence report which exposed him as entirely un-co-operative – declared that he wouldn't pay a fine or accept a community sentence – un-co-operative even to the point of refusing meetings: couldn't be bothered to get up.

He was spoken for by a lawyer – a duty solicitor? – who tried to assure us of his penitence for his taking up of this line – not arrogance, just immaturity, now recognised and surmounted.'

It would have been rash to have put too much weight on this submission from his representative, which, inevitably, did not go beyond bare assertion. We asked the probation officer in court to prepare, or to have prepared, a subsidiary oral report, which might confirm, or not, what we had been told:

'We came back at 2.00 pm – no report. We are told rather pertly that it is 'not policy' to supplement a regular report with an oral update; anyway the speaker had had no time. Is this true, or is she simply anxious not to throw the offender a lifeline? We consider what to do in some perplexity: custody seems the only possible sentence if we proceed to sentence, but should one do so after this refusal by the probation service to help? I start off by thinking we shouldn't but am persuaded otherwise. Just too bad, we feel; he's taken a particular line, after offending, and takes the consequences. We return to court and he's not in the dock, having been taken down to a cell after being disruptive.' (1993)

Finally we sentenced him to twenty-eight days in a Young Offenders' Institution. Looking back, this strikes me as plainly inadequate. We seem to have made the easy and not uncommon mistake of doubting whether custody was appropriate at all – did the facts of the case make it 'so serious'? – deciding that it was so serious, then giving weight to the doubts which we should, at that point, have left behind us and coming to settle on an inadequate term. His lawyer must have gone off reflecting that he'd effectively achieved his object. Certainly, the sentence – very short – was of the kind the Lord Chief Justice of a later date would declare to be one to be avoided.

In the Crown Court, two years later, I found myself dealing with something similar. A young man had been put on probation after an offence of burglary, and had failed to comply with the terms of the probation order:

> '... he should have appeared last Friday but rang to say he was ill. This morning no appearance by him – therefore we issued a warrant – and no medical certificate. He turned up after lunch and was put in a cell. Eighteen years old, said to be looking after his father of eighty-two, and with a son of three. The picture one of a hopeless inability to calculate, of habitual mendacity. The effect of the very lenient sentence last time seemed to have been nil. His appearance jaunty, sulky, defiant – head held at an angle – impression of discontent and viciousness. What to do? We gave him six months in a Young Offenders Institution.' (1995)

Six months is much better than one, if rehabilitation is to be attempted. Even so, it is not very long. Hence the common cry that short sentences are ineffective. This cry usually goes along with the claim that non-custodial alternatives are preferable, even in point of effectiveness. This is a large subject which I cannot discuss here in the fullness it merits. One thing can be said: the conclusion that short sentences are ineffective points quite as clearly to the further conclusion that they should be longer. Would two years have serve the purpose better in this last case?

It is sometimes necessary to sentence an offender who has been remanded in custody for some time before the point of sentence. If he is then given a custodial term, the time spent on remand will be treated as 'served' and deducted from that term. As magistrates' powers are limited, it is quite possible that this will lead to his immediate release. Even in the Crown Court, it may result in his being released quite shortly, often to the indignation of victims and their families, and to protests in the press. This is understandable, but the court's decision is unavoidable. Though a refusal of bail is not a punishment, confinement in prison is likely to be *felt* as a punishment by someone who suffers it. Even the appearance of double punishment is to be avoided. There is a related and often more perplexing problem when someone who has been remanded in custody is then found, on the merits of the case, not to deserve custody, for even a short period, as a punishment. I discuss this in Chapter Six below.

This is not the only way in which Parliament, in enacting bills put forward by the government of the day, probably with very little fuss, as they will be largely uncontroversial, unwittingly makes things difficult. When I was appointed to the bench, in 1989, it was 'good practice', though not obligatory, to get a probation officer's report before passing sentence, except where the case was routine or relatively minor. It was not long before it was made obligatory and not long after that before a report could be dispensed with where a judge or bench was prepared to declare that all the relevant information about the offender was available and that a report would therefore serve no purpose. Here were two changes of tack in a short period. The second change, I have little doubt, can be attributed to pressure from the higher judiciary. The thinking behind the requirement to order a report is easy to see: a court should not make a large intervention in an offender's life without knowing enough about him or her to do so properly. If custody is in question, this seems obvious. Commissioning and obtaining reports, perhaps a month later, does however slow down the whole process. It must be desirable to deal promptly with those who break the law, especially those who offend against public order.

There is also a particular problem for the lay magistracy, acute in cases where the offender has contested the charge and been convicted after a trial. If a report has to be commissioned, it is likely to be difficult in practice to re-assemble the same bench to consider it and pass sentence in its light: it will not be easy to find a day which suits three busy people, and also a defence lawyer, possibly also a prosecutor, which is also one on which the court-staff can find the necessary time and space. The outcome may therefore be that the offender is sentenced by a district judge or by a bench whose members will all have read the report, but of which one member only, or not even one, will have observed him or her during the course of the trial, especially in the witness box.

This difficulty, to which there is no full solution, often came up. It was eased in my later days on the bench, by increased recourse to oral reports from a probation officer, prepared after a brief interview and presented on the same day. Sometimes the probation officer will stand up and say that the interview has shown that a more thorough report is necessary, for which an adjournment will be required. That conclusion has to be accepted. Sometimes, the clerk will point out technical procedural objections. This is part of the clerk's job, though his or her interjection is likely to be registered as unfortunate:

'...the procedural problem of how to sentence a man – I think probably a drug dealer, doing a four-year prison term – for a mass of motoring offences, including failure to stop after an accident and to report [the accident]. I wanted to give short custodial sentences – say, ten days each – for these two, to be consecutive to the four-years. I discovered that dispensing with the preliminary report was impossible for *summary* offences such as these. And who'd have commissioned a report on someone in prison and had him produced in three or four weeks time from a prison in the Midlands? So, in effect, we did nothing but disqualify him [from driving] for three years, so that some of the disqualification would be applicable on his release, presumably after two years.' (1998)

Here was another touch of sophistry. It is possible that he merited three years disqualification on the facts of the case – the *driving* facts – but I doubt it. The one-year which he seemed likely to suffer was more probably right on the facts, but we had to go a roundabout way to bring it about, being impelled to do so by frustration at our inability to pass the sentence which would have increased slightly his time in prison.

The day before this I had been sitting in the Crown Court, along with another justice, with a circuit judge in the chair. At that time, though not now, justices sat in the Crown Court, along with a judge, to pass sentence on matters passed up from below.

'... all we did was sentence two young men – Indians – for stealing from their employer, a firm selling computer software. What they did was manipulate the till so as to take cash when no sale was recorded. The practice seems to have been common and a sudden check was made in January 1997 (!) when these two admitted it. I suspect that if they'd admitted nothing they wouldn't have been charged. The sums stolen were £7,000 and £1,000. I proposed four months and one month respectively, but was voted down. We gave two months and 100 hours CSO [community service order, i.e. unpaid work] respectively. Not enough, but this had been hanging over them for eighteen months. Both students. [The other justice] wouldn't have sent either of them down. The judge proposed the compromise which, I suspect, he'd have imposed if sitting solo' (1998)

Theft from an employer is reckoned to be more serious than plain theft, as it involves a breach of trust. Sentencing for it should therefore be somewhat stiffer. That is common ground but it will be seen from this example that there is likely to be much variation. The court below (a stipendiary magistrate or a bench) must have thought that a custodial term longer than six months, the magistrates' court's limit, should at least be considered: otherwise, why pass it up to the Crown Court? None of the three of us thought of going so far. What weight did we give to the prompt admissions made on detection? I do not say so but I think we must have given some. The three of us sitting together, though we seem to have come to agree with little difficulty, would – if sitting solo – have come up with three different sentences. This last consideration seems to bring out the advantage of having three minds brought to bear on the decision.

Here was a handing-out of punishment which stuck in memory. I am now inclined to think that my lay magistrate colleague was right in thinking that we could properly have spared custody even in the more serious case. I was probably over-influenced by the breach of trust, though there certainly was such. At the time, I would have said that an employee put into a position where a racket was in operation should not only have refused to join in; he should have gone further and informed the employer That is so, but I would now have more sympathy for a young man to whom not splitting on his work-mates probably trumped all other concerns. A stiff community sentence in the more serious case might have been enough. It should be said that our sentence in each case was quite a bit lighter, in its relative brevity, than that which might well have been given, and the custodial sentence probably had a decided deterrent effect once it became known. I have never thought it unjust, but I came to wonder if, on a broader view, it was right.

Something comparable, but decidedly more perplexing is the case where the offender claims that the action in breach of the law for which he or she has to be sentenced was fully justified or at least, in the circumstances, highly excusable. Cases of a gravity which takes them to the Crown Court sometimes catch public attention if the facts of the case provide grounding for this argument. A householder defending his home and, perhaps, his family uses extreme, even lethal, force. Someone in lawful possession of a shotgun uses it against a burglar and kills the burglar or comes close to doing so. Public opinion is usually vociferous and on his side. Magistrates' courts do not deal with cases of this seriousness, but the same argument sometimes comes up. It may occur to the magistrates – it certainly did to me on occasion – even if it is not advanced by an unrepresented defendant.

> 'In the chair in the morning. All went well. The *depressing* quality of so much of the business was however something that came home. Three custodial sentences. One of a woman around forty – West Indian – for ABH on a boy of seven, her stepson. Presented [by the prosecution] as corporal punishment way over the top. She refused legal representation and spoke for herself, quite effectively. A civil servant with no previous convictions. The one plea in mitigation that came through was that such treatment of a child was normal where she came from. Nonetheless she expressed remorse. How to deal with her was a problem. We gave her three months. Lenient, as it could well have been passed up to the Crown Court. Yet I'm not 100% sure we should have sent her to prison for any period...' (2003)

In pleading Guilty to ABH (actual bodily harm), the woman did not use the argument for which I would have been half-prepared, that she thought she was acting rightly in punishing the boy as she did. Suppose she had made that claim? An obvious riposte would have been that she was obliged to obey the law, whether she agreed with it or not, and whether or not she found it surprising. In this context, however, such a riposte would have missed the point. The woman was not asserting that she did not have to obey the law as it was, but seemed to be suggesting to us that the punishment for not obeying it should be mitigated, on the grounds of her background and social conditioning. Should we have found this argument more telling than we did, to the extent perhaps of giving her a conditional discharge rather than custody?

Here is a question which brings up points of much complexity. I am not aware of any general guidance from the appellate courts on the approach to be adopted. In general, magistrates may – and should – consider the character and all the circumstances of those falling to be sentenced: background and social conditioning are a part of that totality, and to exclude them would be arbitrary. On the other hand, to give personal factors very much weight would result in large breaches in the consistency of treatment which justice seems to require. Keeping both considerations in mind is not easy.

The treatment of people's religious beliefs offers a parallel. It is broadly true to say that, in legislation, religious groups are accorded special treatment in respect of minor matters, notably those which do not affect other people adversely. Jews and Muslims are allowed to slaughter animals for food in their own way, which – if there were no such exception – might bring them into breach of the law governing animal-slaughter. Sikh motorcyclists wearing turbans are dispensed from the normal obligation to wear crash-helmets. Such exemptions – especially the first – are not uncontroversial, but they are now well established. This makes it much harder to assert baldly that the law should apply to everyone without exception: it practice, it does not – not altogether. At the same time, public opinion and the policy of prosecutors have in recent years moved strongly against conceding to people of Asian background – husbands and fathers – the rights over their female dependants which, it is said, would have been normal in their countries of origin. Enforced marriage is now seen as an outrage, not to be palliated by reference to background. There is a line which it is often difficult to make out, and it is a shifting one. The principle which appears to govern the drawing of the line, both in popular sentiment and in legislation, seems to be harm to others. This is quite intelligible, and its general adoption explains why some exceptions continue to be controversial, notably animal-slaughter: animals are 'others', at least in being sentient, which seems the main point. The boy, in the case I have described, is certainly covered by 'others'.

I am still unsure whether our decision in this case was right. One thing in its favour, which I have not yet mentioned, will have been its value for deterrence. If the beating of children should be discouraged, that object seems likely to be advanced by the passing of deterrent-sentences. Custody will serve that purpose more effectively than anything else. It is a powerful form of social denunciation. I have however already indicated my reservations of principle over deterrent-sentencing (see Chapter Three). In sum, it amounts to making use of the offender – a dubious procedure, I fear, even if the use is for a good purpose.

Two months later, I was one of a bench which had to deal with an offender who was certainly 'conscientious'.

'... fine enforcement: the usual procession of the sad – inadequate, often illiterate; the shameless, who for no good reason that's evident won't earn a living; the mendacious. One unusual case among this crowd was that of a tall man with a grey beard in his mid-sixties: had been fined for obstructing the highway on a demonstration – £100 and £40 costs. He announced that he refused to pay and wanted to read out a statement. We refused to let him, but the gist was that the Iraq war was criminal and that Blair was a war-criminal who ought to be on trial himself. We ordered him to be searched – £2 odd only found on him. Going down the list of options we established that a distress-warrant would be frustrated: he wouldn't open the door. So we found that we could – and had to – lock him up. We settled on a day's detention, making the 'day' last until 4.30 pm.' (2003)

It is decidedly rare to imprison fine-defaulters, in large part because the law makes it difficult to do so. Every alternative to doing so has to be considered first, as it was here. In this instance the defaulter had come prepared: he had taken care to have no money on him, as the search confirmed. Some loss of liberty was unavoidable. At the same time, I doubt if any court would have wanted to come down hard on the socially harmless and highly conscientious defaulter we had before us, especially as it seemed clear that that was what he wanted, at least at one level. At this distance, I think our disposal of the matter was well-judged, and at the time it seemed to gratify even the would-be 'martyr'. It was of course decidedly lenient, making the point that refusal to pay a fine must attract a penalty but doing no more than just that. In other words, we gave a large discount for conscience.

The sentencing of women has its own problems. It is often claimed that custody is more of a punishment for women than for men, and that women should therefore be spared it even in cases where men might properly receive it. On this view, inconsistency of treatment is justified by a difference in the relevant facts. This claim is most commonly put when the women in question are mothers of young children. It is commonly argued both that women suffer, in a way in which men do not, from the loss of contact, with its accompanying anxiety, and also that the children suffer from being made, for a period, motherless. Here is a line of argument which often goes with another: prison, it is urged, should be reserved for violent offenders and for those who are an immediate threat to others. The two lines of argument come together, as it is claimed that very few women fall into the 'violent offender' category.

The force of the second argument depends very much on how one understands what being 'violent' amounts to. The plain meaning of the word seems to exclude dishonesty, even of the grossest kind, corruption in public office, and even the trafficking of women for prostitution, where this has been founded on deception rather than coercion. These are surely examples of offences where, on conviction, an exemplary sentence is required, which can only be custodial? The first argument is most persuasive when it puts all the emphasis on innocent and vulnerable children: 'if you send her to prison, you're punishing the children'. This must often be a problem for Crown Court judges, but it is also one for magistrates:

> 'A difficult case of a woman who pleads Guilty to driving while disqualified – driving a child to school. This is only two months after disqualification has been imposed. She's also in breach of a probation order and of a CD [conditional discharge]. In effect, everything seems to have been done to mitigate the punitive. Is this now avoidable any longer? But to send a woman with children to prison? We put off decision by remanding her on bail for reports. Adjourn until 15 June, when – I note now – I'm due to sit again.' (1991)

The difficulty in which we found ourselves will be obvious. Driving after having been disqualified from driving has to be taken seriously, as disqualification is the sentence which, as the final sanction, gives the range of penalties for motoring offences their deterrent force. At this time, 1991, imprisonment was the normal, or at least the very frequent, penalty for driving while disqualified. Since then, there has been some relaxation – not, in my view, an obvious change for the better. For quite a few people, disqualification will be catastrophic; it often results in the loss of employment. This in itself will do no one any good, but it does not follow that disqualification does not serve a very useful deterrent purpose, in which it finds its full justification. It is highly plausible to attribute the reduction over the past forty-five years in the incidence of driving 'over the limit' to its employment as the fixed penalty for this offence. For it to have this effect, there has to be, in reinforcement, a heavy sanction for disregarding it – or so it is reasonable to suppose, and this has to be custody.

In this case, the offender had a child (one at least). Here was one consideration, which could have been taken – and was, by us – to point against custody. The apparent alternatives of a probation order and a conditional discharge were effectively ruled out, as they had just been tried and to no effect; indeed the woman had to be sentenced for breaching them. We seem not to have considered a lengthy community service order, or an unpaid work order, as it would be now. With more experience, I think I would have favoured that, but suppose she had then failed to attend or to co-operate? Her record suggested that this was likely. I find it unsurprising, after this interval that we adjourned the hearing for another court to pass sentence. I never discovered the outcome.

I have just touched on the difficulty over agreeing what we take 'violence' to be. In this case, I am unsure, having taken no note, what driving offence had led to the disqualification. It would not have been surprising if this had been driving 'over the limit'. Should seriously bad driving, whether or not on account of having drunk too much, be considered a *violent* act? To count it as such seems to over-extend the normal meaning of the word, even if such driving is as likely to result in serious, even fatal, injury as a typical example of the offence of causing actual bodily harm. If we take the view that women should go to prison only for 'violent' offences, as we often find argued, and also give 'violence' its normal and restricted meaning, we will need to need to justify the non-imprisonment of the dangerous female driver, while the young man who takes a swing at another such goes down for a few months. This does not seem easy.

What of the children? With some discomfort, I am inclined to say that courts should normally take no notice of the circumstances of offenders, including their child-possession or lack of it. This is the line I did take over my career on the bench, especially its later stages. I believe it just has to be accepted that penalties will affect their recipients in greatly differing ways. Imprisonment is calamitous for most people; for a few it would be welcome, as it gives then a roof over their heads. Disqualification from driving is disastrous for quite a few, highly inconvenient for the majority, a matter almost of indifference for someone who does not own a car and who drives only infrequently. It is impossible for a court of law to try to weigh all these factors, for which they would probably have nothing but the offender's word, with the object of equalising punishment.

Where disqualification is the penalty, there is the further objection – a strong one on an egalitarian perspective – that the rich can easily mitigate the consequences, though at the price of spending, or having spent for them, a lot of money. The entrepreneur can arrange for his firm to supply him with a driver; others, less favoured, can take a lot of taxis. This may be regrettable, though the primary purpose – keeping bad drivers off the road, at least for a period, will continue to be met. These cases were endlessly perplexing:

'...a case of driving disqualified. An earlier plea of Guilty. He'd only recently come out of prison, after serving three months for the same offence. Unrepresented – made an effective plea in mitigation on his own account – he was a plumber, had to drive or be driven to do his job and his driver was unavailable or unaffordable. We gave him twenty-eight days and a fine of £250 (twenty-five units at £10), in effect for the main offence and also for driving uninsured. We had some argument before we agreed on this sentence. It seemed to me that *not* to send him down would be to default on our vindicatory function – and be hopelessly inconsistent with the earlier sentence. Yet twenty-eight days after three months – was this consistent? We were strongly affected by his plea insofar as this bore on his circumstances: hence the shortest custodial term that was feasible. And did we take account of the requirement of the last Criminal Justice Act [that of 1991], specifying that one deals with the offence in itself in disregard of the record? This seems to be an example of the practical impossibility of doing this if one's to be rational and consistent and to have a purpose.' (1993)

This brief account exposes all the difficulties. The 1991 Act came into effect, after much discussion, not long after my appointment to the bench. I registered my new colleagues' concern at the prospect of not being able to take an offender's record into account, indeed of not being aware what it was. I recall that, in the event, what seemed to be relevant information was not so comprehensively withheld. It could hardly have been withheld in the case like this without making it impossible for the court to act in a consistent way. Yet, while I absorbed my colleagues' concern, I could well see – and approve of – the Act's foundation in principle in a strict retributivism: the penalty should be strictly what was merited on the facts of the offence – of that offence – and on nothing else.

Looking back, I am as impressed as I was at the time by the lack of consistent intention in dropping the penalty, quite largely, for a recent repetition of the offence. No doubt we were strongly impressed by the offender's account of his circumstances, which I did not record. A plea of that sort can often come over more strongly from someone unrepresented than from even a competent advocate. Even without that, it would have been natural to feel some sympathy for someone who got into trouble while doing no more than earn his living, though the tough-minded could well have pointed out that plumbing is a lucrative business and that its profits should have been enough to have covered his conveyance by taxi for the limited period when it was necessary.

I note from my record that our list on that occasion was one which we took over, at a day's notice, from a stipendiary magistrate who was indisposed. It must be a matter of speculation how she would have disposed of this matter, but I think it likely that the plumber was lucky that he came before us rather than her – if not all that lucky. If I am right in that, here was a nice example of the arbitrariness which I suggested, in chapter one, is a feature of our present way of doing things.

5.

Chair-takers and Clerks

No court will run well if the person presiding over it is not up to the job. What the job consists of is not so easily stated but, as a bare minimum, he or she needs to have a good grasp of procedure and the forcefulness of personality needed to control a court of law; also to be sufficiently clear-headed and articulate to give directions and announce decisions. The closest parallel is with presiding over a large meeting in the world of work. Justices with experience of doing that will have an advantage, though they are likely to find taking the chair in court more demanding. In each case, there is the need to give everyone with a claim to contribute the chance to do so, when called on at the appropriate moment. In court, it is of equal importance to involve, and to be seen to involve, the other two members of the bench when the court is in session, and to lead and guide discussion when the bench has retired to determine its verdict or to consider a bail application or sentence. It is for the chair-taker to bring in the legal advisor as necessary, both in open court and in the retiring room. All this requires experience and judgement rather than prescription. There may be no single good way of presiding over a magistrates' court, but if the job is done badly, this will be obvious and embarrassing.

Taking the chair is demanding and on a busy day may be tiring. It is probably most demanding on those occasions when the court's business is miscellaneous. Our observers in the gallery will have sat through many such busy mornings and marked the variety of things to be done and the speed of dispatch. The list before the bench may cover persons arrested overnight – brawlers, prostitutes or drunken drivers. These can often be dealt with there and then. There will also be defendants who have appeared before, who have been bailed to return so that a further step in the process can be achieved, such as sending the case forward to the Crown Court. There will be those who appear to be sentenced after being remanded on bail for a report. There will be the need to consider whether those who are to be remanded for the first time should be allowed bail or kept in custody. Magistrates have to shift their attention from one piece of business to another, quite different, with barely a moment's pause. Many of those who appear will be represented, and there will be a steady and rather noisy alternation of lawyers in the seats reserved for them. The list-caller manages the sequence of cases like a ringmaster, telephoning to the cells below to call for the production of those detained. The pace is rapid, as it needs to be if the list is to be completed in good time. This can be taxing, more especially for the chair-taker. It is here that the job is more demanding than that of running a large meeting at work, where the business is likely to be familiar and consistent, and where those discharging it are spared the incessant opening and closing of doors and the inescapable undercurrent of whispering.

Presiding over a trial is unlikely to be as demanding as managing the dispatch of a list of this kind, though here it is even more important that attention should never wander. Going through a long list of motoring charges or TV license evasion cases is different again: the work is monotonous, but there is a need to handle with care a succession of unrepresented defendants, many of whom will be inarticulate, with poor English, and ignorant of the law. The chairman, along with the clerk, has to exert himself to see that they are as little disadvantaged as possible – that at least they should have, and feel they have had, a fair hearing. None of this is easy.

While I often sat with chair-takers whom I found not very effective, disaster – that is, public failure and embarrassment – was very rare. The closest approach to it within my own observation came quite early. As I recorded,

'... J— , in the chair, lost control of the court. The defence solicitor opened by blackguarding the prosecutor as representing the Crown Prosecution Service Dirty Tricks Department. This was on the grounds that he'd asked him (the defence) how the defendant meant to plead to an actual bodily harm charge and, on being told Not Guilty, that he'd said he'd substitute a charge... triable summarily only; in effect this would have denied him the option of jury trial. He alleged an 'abuse of process'. This should have been quashed at once with the statement that it's for the prosecution to decide how to proceed. The prosecutor, one of the worst I've seen, rose to the challenge and at one point four or five people were speaking at once, to the general amusement. This over (the prosecutor seeming tacitly to drop – or to defer? – the postulated substitution) the prosecutor tried to resist the previously granted unconditional bail. J— failed to tie him down to indicating changes in the position since this grant and there was a recurrence of slanging. All very embarrassing and evidence of the all-importance of a firm grip by the chair.' (1990)

The long-serving magistrate who, at least on this occasion, was so inadequate in the chair, might – so far as I knew – have been passably competent sitting at the side, as a so-called 'winger'. Not all good magistrates are cut out to be chair-takers.

There would be little point in dealing at length with the respects in which magistrates in the chair sometimes fall short of what is required. I have just suggested what qualities are required, and they are not always found. Almost always, the bench gets through the list despite this. There may even be some compensation in the rough-and-readiness which must sometimes be evident. The comparative speed and smoothness of operation which often characterises district judges doing the same work – perhaps in an adjacent courtroom – may give a bit too much of the opposite impression, the sense of human beings being processed by a machine.

One unhappy occasion is worth describing, as it brings out what the difficulties are. I was sitting as a 'winger' – that is, on one or other side of the chairman – on an occasion when we ran out of work early and took on a case from another court, with which the prosecutor assigned to our court was unfamiliar. The charge was one of criminal damage. This was said to have been done to a door, the property of a man squatting, along with three others, in a house they acknowledged not to be theirs and being pestered, on their own account, by someone representing himself as the owner's agent:

> 'The suggestion was that the person causing the damage had been put up to it by the so-called 'agent'. The case was badly presented, quite unsurprisingly as the prosecutor had had about five minutes to read the papers. I'd noticed that she'd made no attempt to prove that the squatter was the 'owner' of the door – or that he had by some form of extension the rights of ownership which would ground the charge. When we were in the retiring room – adjourned to let the defence consider a document – I remarked on this, saying that ownership looked like being important. There followed an argument with Mrs W— [the chairman], which began cool but became heated. Very unfortunate. I was at a loss, and still am, to see why she objected to the making of points that were pertinent. She's bad in the

chair, being not very sure of procedure, light on basic knowledge of the law...'

What happened next surprised me and, no doubt, also Mrs W—.

'When we went back in, we got a submission of no-case-to-answer. This was not quite my point (no evidence that the door was the property of S— S—) but that the prosecutor had failed to show [that is, to put in evidence that] the defendant had acted without 'proper authority' – an element in the definition of the offence. The clerk came in at this point, surprisingly (to me) in sympathy with the defence. This line was then supported by the more senior clerk called in.'

I went on to comment:

'It seems to drive a large hole through the restraints on direct action against squatters if a prosecutor has to demonstrate 'beyond reasonable doubt' that an owner did not give such authority. I very much wonder if this is right. The point seems to be made for reference to the Divisional Court. So we declared we found no case to answer and added that we had it in mind to bind the defendant over. This we then did, Mrs W— not handling it very well... To the squatters sitting at the back we must have looked like an unprepared gaggle, too much and too obviously in the hands of the clerks.'

I was sharply aware of what was discreditable in our handling of this trial, though in a longer perspective I have more sympathy for Mrs W— than I showed in the record from which I have quoted: a tricky point of law, or more than one such point, had come up without warning, and I suspect she was flustered. It would have been better to have allowed a longer break before we started the trial, giving the prosecutor more time to absorb the facts and to consider their implications, and giving ourselves the opportunity to brief ourselves, with the clerk's assistance, on the legal framework. That we failed to proceed this way was as much my responsibility as that of my colleagues.

Later that day, a further point struck me:

> ' … the damage allegedly done was to a chipboard cover to an existing hole in the door, stuck to the door from the inside. I suspect that this chipboard was certainly the property of the squatter who put it there. Could we not have taken this by itself to be the 'locus' of the offence [so disposing of my original doubt]? Or is chipboard stuck to a door no longer a discrete item?' (1996)

Reflection of this kind shows how readily points of dispute which seem to relate to the law can turn out to be conceptual. What constitutes a door? Is a patch on a door a part of it or a distinct addition to it? The case was troubling in several ways, and I have little doubt now that we were well advised to end it as we did.

In 1990, at the time of the fiasco I have described above, the bench was in course of bringing in a new procedure for selecting justices for the chair. Up to then, taking the chair had gone with seniority of service, sometimes, if rarely, with consequences of the kind I have described. Under the new procedure, a small committee of the whole bench was appointed to select court chairmen or 'presiding justices'. Not all justices want to become chair-takers, but most do. Failure to be selected for the position is likely to be resented. The new arrangements for selection were attended by acrimony and it was some time before they were fully accepted. As a newcomer, I could observe this from the side and feel thankful that I was not involved. I observed too something of the self-interest and self-importance which, in a few cases among my colleagues, seemed to go with undertaking the work of a magistrate. This was sometimes discomfiting.

Commonly, when the magistrate in the chair is ineffective, the clerk will try to supply his or her deficiencies. Usually, this amounts to no more than giving a tactful reminder or saying in open court something of significance which the chairman has omitted to say or expressed poorly. In a case of unusual weakness, such as the one from 1990 recorded above, assistance from the clerk might amount to taking over the direction of the court. This is an unhappy solution, if only because a clerk who is doing the chairman's job will have too little attention left for his own. A poor solution is however plainly preferable to none. It is better to have the 'wrong' person controlling the court than no one.

In 1989 there were around a dozen clerks in my petty sessional division, to act as legal advisors to the justices and to provide them with support in court. They also sat with the stipendiary magistrates, but only to provide administrative support, as the stipendiaries (now styled district judges) were legally qualified and deemed not to need advice. The clerks also had work to do outside the courtroom, in the processing of cases through the system. At each of the division's two courthouses there was a senior clerk, to whom lay magistrates could appeal if they wanted a second view of the advice of the court clerk *cum* legal advisor. Most clerks were barristers or solicitors, more often the latter, but some had qualified for the job by gaining a certificate in magisterial law after a course at a polytechnic. Current policy is to require all clerks to have a full legal qualification, in time cutting out this last class. This seems an unnecessary change. It is not easy to see why passing examinations in such fields of law as real property or contract should enhance a clerk's ability to advise lay magistrates on points of criminal law or procedure. The point of the new requirement is, no doubt, that a court clerk should be of the intellectual capacity to gain a full legal qualification. There is obvious force in this, though my own very narrow experience was that the few clerks without this qualification were no less effective. Clerks who are legally qualified should at least be more mobile, equipped to move, if they should come to wish to, to different employment in the law, though I would not expect the very narrow experience of working in a magistrates' court to have much 'transfer value'.

Until well into the twentieth century, it was possible for clerks, who were usually local solicitors, to be part time. Their successors are now full-time, with a wide span of responsibility, discharging their advisory role in the court room through a staff of assistants. It is these assistants whom magistrates think of and deal with as 'the clerks', though the favoured term is now 'legal advisors', which is certainly more clearly descriptive. More recently, clerks have, in effect if not in form, become quasi civil servants as staff of Her Majesty's Courts and Tribunals Service (HMCTS).

It was not long before I came to appreciate that it was as important to establish a good working relationship with the clerks as with my colleagues, and to find that this would not always be easy. It must be even less easy for the clerks to get on to the appropriate terms with a much larger number of magistrates, in particular those of them, about half the total, who take the chair in court. Some of these will be only too happy for their court clerk to take on as much of the role of running the court as he properly can, or rather more than that; others will resent this and see it as a usurpation. A balance has to be struck here and no two individuals will strike it in quite the same place. If it is not struck, the outcome will be unhappy and all too obvious, as each party tries to impose itself. This is not just a matter of temperament and natural assertiveness, or the lack of it. The clerk has a duty to see that business is conducted properly, and this may require him or her to intervene, whatever the consequences for some ineffective chairman's sense of propriety. Doing justice has to come first.

The role of a Justices' Clerk – and , by extension, that of his assistants, the court clerks – has a basis in statute: it is not just a matter of local practice or convention, though what is now laid out in statute can easily be seen to be the end-product of a long development. The Courts Act 2003 summarises his or her prime functions as being to advise the justices on the law (including procedure and practice) and to bring points of law to their attention. The role is not simply reactive. A more detailed account of it was to be found in a Practice Direction from the Lord Chief Justice reissued in 2002. This made it clear that everything said about the Justices' Clerk applies to his assistants. It is these assistants who now, in almost all respects, do the job – that is, who sit in court and who are available for advice outside court. Over my twenty years on the bench, the Justices' Clerk became an ever more remote figure, with a wider span of responsibility, towards the end of this period accommodated in a different building, and available for consultation only over the telephone. This appeal by telephone must have been very rare; in my own experience it never happened. The dozen or so clerks in one or other of our two courthouses had their own grading structure and it was not unusual for a beginner to appeal for support or confirmation to someone more senior, either at his or her own initiative or at the prompting of members of the bench. The Justices' Clerk, in fact, has come to be promoted out of the discharge of the primary function. In this respect, he resembles a headteacher.

The Practice Direction goes on to define the court clerk/ legal advisor's role more precisely. To instance only what is most important, it consists of giving advice on the law and on questions on mixed law and fact, though not of making judgements of fact, of asking questions of the parties to a case or of witnesses with a view to clarifying the evidence, though not of cross-examining them, and of helping an unrepresented defendant to present his or her case, though without slipping into being an advocate. Asking clarifying questions and helping the unrepresented and the possibly vulnerable are functions which fall also to the chairman of a bench, and it will be evident that there is the risk of a clash in their discharge. It is for the chairman to run the court, but the clerk's role is so varied and extensive that, without a due measure of tact on the clerk's part, the casual observer – our friend in the gallery, let us say – may think it is for the clerk, at least on occasion. It is unsurprising that some observers go away thinking that the clerk is the one who counts.

It is not only for the chairman to develop a good working relationship with the clerk of the day; those who sit at the side, the so-called 'wingers', need to know when and how the clerk should be called in to advise them. This came home to me early in my time on the bench, when I came to reflect on my second day of sitting in court: 'a surprisingly interesting day', I recorded, though it was given over to traffic matters, not often found interesting. A small point seemed to open up a field of doubt:

> '... a Not Guilty plea to breaching provisional driving licence conditions [driving without L-plates] on the grounds that the defendant had at that time an International Driving Licence – no doubt about the breach otherwise. This last document was produced and looked odd – possibly tampered with, apparently incoherent. As the defence rested on it, we convicted. The trouble was that the prosecution had challenged it in no way – if it had

and had exposed doubts like ours (first raised by me) the doubts might have been allayed.'

In other words, the defendant might have had a good explanation for the 'oddity' of the document he presented, but did not offer it because he was left unaware of what was in our minds. This should have worried me, though at the time it did not. Perplexity came later and spread more widely :

'Behind this is the general point of the right of justices to consider points which seem to come out of the evidence but which have not been put to them [explicitly]. Points which seem to favour the defence but not those which favour the prosecution? If not this, is there not a risk of wrongly convicting the innocent? I need to get a feel for the circumstances in which justices can put their own questions.' (1989)

I was sufficiently concerned by this point to raise it out of court with the chief clerk soon afterwards:

'He suggested that we could have checked that the prosecution had seen the International License and could have asked the defendant to explain any oddities, conceding that we'd have [had] no alternative but to take any plausible explanation.'

This was good advice, applicable more widely. On the narrower point with which I had been concerned at the time, he explained the law in a way which surprised me:

'He said, though, that a driver with a provisional licence was bound by its terms even if he had an International Licence. We were not told this by our clerk ....'

In other words, the defendant's possession of an International

Licence was no defence to the charge put to him, even if its validity was unquestionable. It is easy to be wise with hindsight, and it now strikes me that I should have at least suspected that this would be the law: otherwise a driver from abroad might have two licences of overlapping scope, and in case of difficulty could produce whichever one suited him. I concluded my record, no doubt with a sense of embarrassment: '[the chief clerk's advice] suggests that we found the right verdict if not for the right reason.'

These first few sittings on the bench made it plain that obtaining advice on the law would not always be a simple matter, also that a court clerk's advice would sometimes be unsound. There was nothing startling in this last recognition: everyone sometimes makes mistakes in his or her work. There is however a difficulty for the lay magistrate, concerned to pull his weight in a field unfamiliar to him, who may on occasion suspect unsoundness and mistrust what he is told. I soon learned from the reaction of those with whom I was sitting, at this early stage always more experienced than I, that I would have little support – rather the opposite – in questioning a clerk's advice. There were occasions , not very frequent, where doing this seemed unavoidable: the advice seemed perhaps to contradict that of another clerk, on the same point of law, given on another occasion. But was it indeed the same point of law, and might there not be differences of fact to explain the difference of advice? More seriously, the advice we had been given might seem, not indeed at all often, to point to a decision which would jar with basic notions of fairness. I was not so naive as to suppose that this would invalidate the advice – I had after all made my career in the civil service – but I wanted to be quite sure that the law was such that there was indeed no alternative.

The speed at which magistrates' work has to be done is alone enough to make it difficult for the beginner on the bench to pursue such lines of inquiry as these. I found that they were likely to be met by a hiss from the side, if the court were in session, to the effect that, 'we always take our clerks' advice' or that, 'we can talk about that later if you want to'. This made me aware that I was being found a difficult colleague. If I had said simply that I wanted to raise the level from which we were taking advice, and therefore to retire to consult someone more senior, I would have been acting within my rights. I would have been wiser to do this oftener, though in so doing I would still have been judged to be delaying matters and imperilling the completion of our day's work. This would have been resented. The problem here has no comfortable solution. The newly appointed justice is fully responsible from the start, and the decision of the bench is formally as much his or hers as that of its other, more experienced, components. Everyone newly appointed has to decide how far to acquiesce without fuss in decisions where both the reasoning involved and the consequences are less than fully clear to him. I quite often did so acquiesce and walked away afterwards with some discomfort.

How should the beginner take the insistence that 'we always take the advice of our clerks'? As 'we' do not unfailingly do so in practice, let us assume that what is meant by this is that we *should* always do so. This may be urged on the grounds that it would be rash not to do so, as someone without legal education is at least very much less likely to be right on a point of law than someone with it. It may mean – also or instead – that it would be rash to disregard a clerk's advice because, in the event of a successful appeal to the High Court against their decision, magistrates who insisted on doing so might be made personally liable for costs, which would probably be substantial. It may mean no more than that the system on which magistrates' courts operate would be disturbed if justices did anything other than take their clerks' advice. I was told briskly in my early days on the bench, 'Don't question the advice. If you do, you'll get less help, not more.'

There is force in all these thrusts, though not much in the threat of being made liable for costs. How often does this happen, I wonder? So far as I can gather, a costs order against lay magistrates will be made only when they have been pig-headed. The commonest case of this seems to be when a magistrates' court has to sentence a motorist for driving after taking alcohol over the prescribed limit. For this offence, disqualification from driving for at least twelve months is normally obligatory. It is however open to the court to find what are called 'special reasons' for not disqualifying him. The term, 'special reasons' is a term of art. If the bench insists on finding 'special reasons' after the clerk has made clear the narrowness of its definition, the prosecution may well appeal, if only to prevent their decision leading to a widening of the definition and so to a weakening of the deterrent effect of the law. It is in such cases as these that the High Court has awarded costs against magistrates. I am unaware of any recent instance of the court's doing so where magistrates have disregarded their clerk's advice on a contentious point, where the law may not have been settled or clear, prompted to do so by their sense of fairness.

The opposite seems more likely. In a case from the mid-nineties, which was widely reported, a lay bench in Lincoln which had committed a woman to prison for non-payment of council tax was criticised by the High Court in trenchant, even scathing, terms. I rely on contemporary accounts and on my memory for the facts of the matter. It seems that the magistrates had been advised by their court clerk – wrongly – that they no alternative but to commit her. They were unable to raise the level of advice, as it appears that no one more senior was accessible. With the benefit of hindsight, they should have adjourned the case until someone was. Everything about this suggests that the magistrates had absorbed all too thoroughly the precept that a clerk's advice should not be questioned and that they feared the consequences for themselves of refusing to take it.

It struck me at the time that the High Court's treatment of the matter was highly salutary. What it seemed to make clear was that magistrates were finally responsible for what they did and that they should not be on the bench if they were unwilling to accept this responsibility and act accordingly. In unusual and happily infrequent circumstances this could be very awkward. So be it. Here was a good riposte to the calls for caution and conformity which one is likely to register when starting on the bench.

I should not give the impression that magistrates are at all often inclined to disregard their court clerks' advice, especially where this is endorsed by a Justices' Clerk or by his or her deputy. Nearly always, a clerk's advice is unsurprising and, on the face of it, offering no grounds for dissent, at least from those without legal qualifications. If advice is given during the course of a trial or at its conclusion, before the bench retires, it is likely to be uncontested by the legal representatives on either side, the argument between the two sides being on points of fact only. Obviously, this concordance strengthens one's trust in its soundness. It can be awkward when a clerk comes in with advice inconveniently late in the course of proceedings, when it has taken time for him or her to appreciate that it is necessary. Sometimes too the advice will be modified – effectively changed – after the legal representative on either side has drawn attention, late in the day, to some relevant precedent.

What is much more of a problem is advice from a clerk which may cut against the magistrates' ability to do substantive justice.

I recall the occasion when I was advised not to consult the street atlas which I had brought with me, for that purpose, into court. This came in the course of a trial for a motoring offence, probably that of 'driving... without due care and attention'. It is often hard for magistrates to follow the evidence in such cases, as witnesses may struggle to explain how one street relates to another, when three or four streets may come together within a small area. A waving of arms about may not convey very much. This is something which may need to be clear if the bench is to come to understand how a collision came about and whose fault it was. To keep open on the bench the relevant page of the A to Z street atlas is usually enough to make what is being said comprehensible. To be advised by the court clerk to close it was therefore more than disconcerting. His advice was effectively a direction as it was given in open court, with a witness in the box. The circumstances ruled out discussion, and the point did not seem so important that we had to retire. When I questioned the advice afterwards, I was told that I should not try to give evidence to myself. One can see that – on any strict view – consulting a street atlas counts as giving evidence to oneself, when it has not been put in as evidence by either side. It is clear too that the principle appealed to has an obvious soundness. But its adoption in the sort of case we were dealing with was not going to help us do substantive justice, rather the opposite.

Sometimes there a point comes up on which the law is plainly unsettled. I recall the trial of a woman for driving uninsured and without a valid licence She had failed to respond to the summons and we were proceeding in her absence:

> 'It was clear that she'd failed to produce an insurance policy – but was it clear that she'd been asked to produce it? If the charge had been 'failure to produce', this question would have been manifestly to the point: was it so in the case of a charge of not

having one, once she'd been charged with this, where we were clear – as we were – that she'd been driving? The prosecutor said that the onus was on the defendant to produce the policy once driving had been proved and quoted Wilkinson [the text-book authority] at us. The clerk, Miss C—, demurred and said that 'at this court' it had been held that the Crown had to show that production had been required at the time. We thought it likely – in the retiring room – that 'at this court' meant just that that was D—'s [the chief clerk's] view – one that he's impressed on the clerks. We therefore thought that we'd better get D— to join us and I got the prosecutor to repeat her line in open court and him to say why he differed. We then, with some hesitation, but unanimously, agreed with the prosecutor and convicted. D— told us that there's a similar case waiting for a Divisional Court hearing – no doubt appeal by the Crown against a verdict in line with D—'s view.' (1997)

This was not the end of the matter. A few weeks later I was taken aside by the chairman of the bench – that is, of all eighty or ninety of us – who had been asked by D— to tackle me on the subject of our omission to act in line with his advice. Having been the chairman on the earlier occasion, I must have seemed to be the one to be spoken to. This was an inept way to proceed and advanced matters little. It prompted me to write to D— and to copy the letter to the chairman of the bench and my two colleagues. I said that on a point where the law was unsettled, it must be open to magistrates to form their own view of the cogency of arguments put to them. The inexpert in any field can usually have a fair stab at appraising the arguments of experts: public life would hopelessly inhibited if this were not so. There were no further repercussions, though there might have been: it now seems to me odd that I never tried to discover how the High Court disposed of the matter then awaiting its attention – or that no one made a point of informing me. On the point which had perplexed us I continued to be in a state of uncertainty.

There were grounds for reflection on what had happened on this occasion. I was conscious that D— was highly efficient professionally, and had no doubt that he had been concerned that a bench to which he was the legal advisor should not find a charge proved when it ought not to be. Was this all that lay behind it? I was aware in myself, in my discharge of a magistrate's role, of the satisfaction of having power – however small its sphere – and I thought I could observe this satisfaction in those I sat with and in those who advised us. One ground for choosing this form of public service over others may be at least a fair degree of authoritarianism of personality. Throughout my time on the bench I thought I could observe this strand in the motivation of many of my colleagues and in that of some of our legal advisors, along of course with much else that was more disinterested. Knowing myself better than any of them, I did not take myself to be without it.

Strains in the working relationship between lay magistrates and their legal advisors are not unusual. Quite a few of my colleagues had had difficult passages with D—. In my own case, I found that any strains and tensions between myself, when I took the chair, and our legal advisor of the day became fewer in number and more easily managed as I gained in experience. I fancied that as the clerks came to feel confident that I would not mishandle the management of the court, the discharge of their own role became more effective and more easily accommodated. In other words, we worked together more effectively as we came to be better acquainted. This is probably the only ready way to get over an inevitable difficulty. It makes a good argument for not having benches which are too large for personal acquaintanceship to develop.

Lay magistrates have often been supposed to be too much in the hands of their clerks. In a book published before the Second World War under the pseudonym, 'Solicitor', to which I will refer again, we find this common judgement supported by examples. I often found myself wondering how far, if at all, this dependence was to be found at my own court within my own time and also – not quite the same question – how the relationship impressed the miscellany of people who passed through the gallery. This was not an easy question to answer, as the over-dependence, if there was such, would have varied as particular justices and particular clerks were brought into a working relationship. Some partial answers are possible. My own experience was that court clerks were nearly always scrupulous in leaving questions of fact to those whom they advised, and generally discreet in advising them on their sentencing powers, a role in which there would have been scope for advice to slip into direction. This was all the more notable, and creditable, as I recall magistrates who would have been only too willing to be told what to do by the clerk. There were occasions, in the retiring room, where the need was to determine a verdict, where the evaluation of evidence was difficult, when there was a bleat from the side, usually from someone newly appointed, to the effect that we should ask the clerk what he or she made of it. This showed only that there were some members of the bench uncomfortable with the responsibility they had chosen to assume. Where magistrates are weak or otherwise ineffective – perhaps simply in not knowing enough – it is likely that the clerks will to some degree take over their role.

Legal advisors need not only to be of the right intellectual capacity but also to be of the right bent. They have to be able to work as members of a team, concerned along with others to do things in a proper way. This calls for a certain temperament. Qualities of self-assertiveness which may be useful and appropriate in many another sphere may be detrimental in this one. I sometimes wondered why X... or Y... had not gone into private practice at the Bar or as a solicitor, where he or she might have made more money and found more satisfaction. The reason why is probably to be found in the security and regularity of pay to be found in working for Her Majesty's Courts and Tribunals Service (HMCTS). Salary levels appear to be sufficient, at least at present, to recruit people of the right capacity. Legal advisors are sometimes appointed district judges, and I know of at least one who was appointed further, to be a circuit judge, sitting in the Crown Court. Taken as a whole, the calibre of legal advisors seemed to me to be high, more notably so in 2009, when I retired, than in 1989, when I was sworn in. For all its strains, I do not take the provision for justices to get legal advice, as it is now, to be a weakness in the system.

6.

Bail and Warrants

Persons in the public eye who are supposed to have broken the law are sometimes said by the fair-minded to be 'innocent until proved guilty'. As expressed, this makes little sense, but the employment of some such form of words is revealing. It is a maladroit way of expressing the widespread conviction that no one should be held to be guilty of a crime, still less punishable for it, until he or she has admitted guilt or been convicted after a trial. Guilt should not be presumed, and we will catch that common intuition and express it much more clearly if, instead of the words quoted, we say 'not to be treated as guilty until proved guilty'. So expressed, this states a principle of the first importance.

The grant of bail to those to be remanded, or its withholding, has to be considered with this principle in mind. Let us suppose that someone is produced in court after being arrested. The court will not be ready to proceed with the trial – if there is to be a trial – and the defendant will probably want legal advice, or at least full details of what is alleged. An adjournment will be inescapable. The question then comes up: what should be done with the person in the dock? He or she will almost certainly hope to receive an unconditional grant of bail – that is, to be able to walk free and to do so without conditions, simply noting the date of the next hearing. A remand in custody must be most disagreeable in itself and confinement in prison may make it harder to prepare a defence. Bail with conditions is greatly preferable to being taken off to prison in a van, though the conditions imposed by the court – that is, limitations on his freedom of action – may be vexatious. He may, for instance, be required to surrender his passport. How far is treatment of this kind compatible with the hardly controversial principle just stated, on which he is 'not to be treated as guilty until proved guilty'? What is the justification for restricting his liberty in the way the prosecution may propose, or which may occur spontaneously to the court, when – so far – he has been convicted of nothing?

The answer to such questions has to be that he is not being treated as *guilty* before being found guilty, but rather that he is the object of an administrative decision which has to be justified on largely pragmatic grounds. Whether or not it can be justified is for a court of law to decide. The decision is administrative rather than strictly judicial, though it will be taken within a judicial context by judges or magistrates. Here is the inescapable awkwardness in the position of those who must take the bail decision: they should not prejudge, but they are bound to take account of what they will be told.

There is a presumption in favour of unconditional bail, to be found in statutory form in the Bail Act of 1976. Only in the case of a few very serious offences is this reversed, with the presumption being in favour of custody. A grant of bail permits the defendant to live freely, within the limits of any conditions which may be attached to it, with the obligation – always – to surrender to the court at a future date, which is specified. It is a breach of the Act – that is, a criminal offence – to fail to surrender or to be late in doing so. The presumption is not however irrebuttable. There are frequently occasions where either the facts of the case, as stated by the prosecutor, or the circumstances of the defendant, or both, point to refusing bail or to granting it only on conditions. The court has to do what it can to ensure that a defendant attends court as required on future occasions, in particular for his trial. It hardly needs saying that many defendants expect to be convicted; if they expect also to be sentenced to imprisonment, they will have a strong motive not to present themselves. There may be grounds here for making an exception to the presumption. A remand in custody will secure attendance. The attachment of conditions to bail will not do that, but it may sufficiently address the risk of the defendant absconding . One or other of these options may seem unavoidable.

The court may also suspect that the defendant would commit offences if allowed his liberty. This last consideration is often expressed in terms of his committing *further* offences, an unhappy expression, as it seems to imply that he has certainly offended on the present occasion. The court should avoid pre-judging that, but it may be unable to avoid drawing adverse conclusions from his record, which the prosecutor will produce if he opposes unconditional bail. This may show that the defendant is – or at least has been – a professional criminal. It may also suggest that he is a drug addict, who is likely to be in need of funds to fund a habit, which may be unobtainable honestly. If it does, it is bound to seem quite likely – to say the least – that he will offend.

A third exception may derive from the need to ensure that there is no interference with the course of justice, for instance by interfering with witnesses or threatening someone whose recourse to the police has prompted the prosecution. There may be others, such as to ensure the defendant's own security, whether from gang violence or from an outraged public opinion.

To find an exception, such as these, the court has to be satisfied that there are grounds for doing so. Typical grounds, such as a defendant's record, have also been mentioned already. Where a defendant has breached bail on previous occasions, or committed offences when on bail, there will seem to be strong grounds for remanding him in custody or at least for imposing stringent conditions of bail, such as daily reporting to a police station or the provision of one or more sureties. The court is obliged to give its consideration this shape, as a form has to be completed with detail of both the exception or exceptions and, in the case of each, the grounds for finding it. While the distinction of exception and grounds for making it is not hard to state, it is not always easy to observe. I recall sometimes finding myself coming to the view that X should not have bail because he was the person he was, as evidenced by the way he habitually behaved, as evidenced by the record. Forcing this conclusion into the prescribed format may require artificial distinctions.

Remand in custody is a necessary evil, quite often unavoidable. It is an evil because, though it is not an anticipation of sentence, it may feel like that to the person remanded and it is likely to hamper the preparation of his defence. It is expensive, because maintaining prisons is expensive, and it aggravates the overcrowding of prisons, which is at present notorious. It will sometimes have the odd effect of making the custodial sentence which a defendant may eventually receive, on conviction, seem inordinately short. I discussed that in Chapter Four, where I pointed out that that was not the only awkwardness. In 1994, after sitting in the Crown Court, with a circuit judge in the chair, to deal with committals for sentence, I recorded that we gave a youth of eighteen a combination order for burglary – that is, the combination of unpaid work and supervision by the probation service. The offender had been remanded in custody for the previous four months. I recorded nothing of the facts of the matter, so cannot now say that our sentence seems questionable. In all likelihood, it was right and proper. It was plainly intended to be constructive and, taken by itself, would have seemed lenient. From the offender's point of view, however, it must be plainly unfair when what is formally a lesser sentence than custody affects him much more disagreeably than a custodial sentence would have done. In this instance, if the offender had been sentenced to youth custody for eight months or less, he would have 'walked free'.

It is therefore unsurprising that defence advocates sometimes seek to persuade magistrates to pass a custodial sentence, when there are obvious and more lenient alternatives. Magistrates often fall in with this proposal, moved no doubt by the wish to avoid excessive severity. In doing so, they breach the principle that a custodial sentence should only be given when it is merited – that is, that the offence is 'so serious', to employ the formula, that custody is inescapable. They then have to declare for the record why they found this to be so in the case before them. This can always be done, with a modicum of ingenuity. In other words, they sometimes fall into sophistry, and when I say 'they' I include myself.

For one reason or another, bail is often withheld. In my time on the bench, I found that I was a party to this decision much more frequently than I joined in passing a custodial sentence on someone Guilty of an offence. The decision to remand a defendant in custody might be more perplexing – and in that sense harder – but it seemed easier to take as it was not, at least formally, punitive. It was less likely to prompt the self-questioning which, at least in my own case, often followed the painful decision to send someone to prison by way of sentence. For the person concerned, this may have been a distinction in principle only: the reality of what follows will be much the same in each case, and so will such likely consequences as loss of employment. In the past, the conditions of confinement were notably less onerous for those in custody on remand. This was as it should be, and it is regrettable that it is now barely the case. Those on remand used to be permitted to have their own food sent in, but are no longer. One worthwhile distinction from those who have been sentenced seems to be that those on remand are not obliged to do prison work, though this may mean simply that they spend even more time in their cells. Another, which is certainly valuable, is that they enjoy easier visiting conditions

Every now and again, there is a glimpse of what remand in custody can amount to for the person remanded. The Australian, Julian Assange, surrendered to the police in December 2010, after the authorities in Sweden had sought his extradition for questioning after allegations of his having committed rape or near-rape. As Assange was notorious for his leading role in the WikiLeaks exposure of government information, what followed was widely reported. The question for the court was whether he should have bail pending the extradition hearing. This was refused at the first application and he was remanded to Wandsworth prison. In the course of a renewed application, his solicitor claimed, to quote from a report in the Press, that 'he was in solitary confinement for twenty-three hours a day with access to only a tabloid newspaper'. Conditions were described, in one account, as 'Dickensian', in another as 'Orwellian'. The language used smacks of hyperbole, but we may still suppose that Assange, like many others who make no such headlines, suffered what is effectively punishment, when all that is justifiable on pragmatic grounds is such loss of liberty as is necessary to ensure attendance at court or some other object of importance

The alternative to remand in custody is bail, with or without conditions. Conditions attached to bail are intended to eliminate or reduce identified risks – of which I have given instances above – and should be proportionate to that object. Magistrates and judges have a free hand in prescribing conditions. In unusual circumstances, these may need to be ingenious. Typical bail conditions are to report to the police at specified times, to keep away from a designated house or street or district, so as to reduce the risk of accidental (or pretended-accidental) contact with an alleged victim or other witness, and to live and sleep at a designated address, usually that of a friend or relative, with the same intention and also with the intention of ensuring that the police know where the person bailed is to be found. There is a tendency among lay magistrates, which sometimes prevails, to impose conditions almost for their own sake. This may betray a deeper tendency to regard a defendant as properly punishable in advance of trial. Only self-awareness on the magistrate's part will correct this.

Someone on bail does not commit a criminal offence simply in breaking a condition: judges and magistrates are not legislators. He or she is however liable to be arrested and produced in court if he does so. The earlier decision to grant bail will then be reconsidered and may be overturned. There may of course be a good excuse for the breach – say, the house prescribed for his residence caught fire – or one which is arguably good – say, that he needed to find a teenage daughter who was overdue home. If there is no good excuse or none that can be substantiated, bail may be, and often is, withdrawn and he will be remanded in custody. Sometimes there have been not merely a breach but, on the face of it, something which amounted to a criminal offence in itself. It may be, for instance, that he did not simply contact a witness (a breach of the condition), but that he tried to intimidate him or her (a breach of the law). Withdrawal of bail will then almost always follow.

It may be made a condition that family-members or friends, possibly several, put up sureties – that is, make themselves liable to forfeit money, perhaps a great deal, if there is a breach of bail by the defendant – if, for instance, he absconds. When sureties have been taken and the defendant then absconds, the court may well be faced with a painful difficulty. The rationale for the surety process is that someone, or more than one person, assumes responsibility for the defendant's presentation of himself at court at the prescribed time. The surety is backed by a specified sum, which those offering it stand to forfeit if the person bailed defaults. Forfeiture seems to be fair, if we hold that those offering sureties have fallen down on an obligation they chose to assume, in awareness of the risk. The trouble with this view of the matter is that it seems to be grounded in an older social order than the one we now inhabit. In the past it would have seemed natural for a parent to take on this responsibility and for the world around him to give support. The necessary degree of control might then have been feasible. It must be a question whether these conditions still obtain.

It is part of the court's duty in granting bail and taking a surety for attendance to investigate the financial resources of the person offering it. In the event of default by the person bailed, the court does not have to take the full amount from those who made themselves responsible, but the full amount should be there to be taken. It is usually necessary to adjourn the hearing for the necessary check to be made. Sometimes it turns out later that this has not been done adequately:

> 'We had to decide how much of a surety of £5,000 to take after the bailee absconded: a nice and, I should think, truthful West Indian couple, who couldn't possibly have done what they'd pledged themselves to do, which was to 'deliver' their son of thirty-one. We 'forfeited' £500, ie 10% – I argued for £1,000. This shows up the very doubtful usefulness of the surety mechanism.' (1998)

It should have been evident at an earlier stage that natural parental concern might prompt the offer of a surety well outside the resources of those offering it. It may have been that the parents demonstrated that they had house-property of a value sufficient to cover the risk. This is hardly good enough: no court will wish to enforce the sale of the family house in order to recover a mere fraction of its value. What those offering sureties need to have is 'liquid' funds ample enough for the full sum at risk to be supportable. Was our decision on this occasion to take only a small part of what had been offered the right one? It was certainly an unhappy one, if inescapable. If it becomes common knowledge that in practice something less than the whole sum will be taken, it may become too tempting to offer too much.

Those who have to take bail decisions are unlikely to discover their outcome. The district judge or magistrates who accepted the offer of what turned out to be an unobtainable surety will not, in all likelihood, have discovered how it turned out. On rare occasions, an unhappy outcome may become notorious, and those who have given bail may have their misjudgement in doing so exposed to the world. In 2005, a bench sitting in south London gave bail with conditions to Michael Pech, charged with threatening and harassing a woman. One of the conditions was, unsurprisingly, not to contact her in any way. Some six months later, after Pech had returned home to the Czech Republic to obtain a firearm, he went to the department store where the woman was working, and shot and killed her and then himself. The cry, 'Why did they let him out?' was prominent in the welter of comment and protest which followed. This question was readily answerable: the decision to give Pech bail, though plainly mistaken in the light of what happened, may have been perfectly reasonable in the light of what was known of him at the time. Any court's decisions on bail will sometimes be seen to have been ill-judged, and very occasionally a grant of bail will have consequences as bad as in the case of Pech. Magistrates charged with the responsibility for making this decision – that is, on occasion, all magistrates – need to be clear-headed and not over-sensitive on their own account. A storm of public criticism, justified or – more likely – not, is one of the liabilities of the job.

Magistrates cannot be right all the time. What is unsatisfactory, yet in practice hard to correct, is that there is no provision for making them aware of plainly mistaken decisions, when these become apparent. In the world outside the courtroom, magistrates may from time to time, as individuals, have to take decisions equally difficult. In these other instances they will almost always be able to see in due course whether those decisions were soundly based. This makes it possible to learn from experience, and to hope to judge matters better in future. In respect of bail decisions, there is no such opportunity. A magistrate, looking back, hardly ever has any idea whether someone given bail has presented himself for trial. To set up a system for conveying such notification must be feasible, but it could not be brought about without some cost. The cost may be, and would certainly be argued to be, disproportionate to the benefit. More often than not, magistrates would remember too little of the circumstances which conditioned their decision to be able to draw useful conclusions, beyond the obvious one, where there had been many defaults, that they needed to be more robust.

In my early days on the bench, I was inclined to agonise over bail decisions. I find I developed a brisker style in time and with experience:

> 'Several bail decisions – one, a man is due to appear tomorrow charged with a Bail Act breach: do we give him bail until tomorrow? Will he threaten – again, it's alleged – a witness (a girl of sixteen)? We decide not to run the risk.' (1992)

'... so difficult are these bail decisions: he'd been arrested in June and released on bail, arrested again in August for the same thing [driving after having been disqualified] plus driving over the limit. All charges to be vigorously contested, we were told ...'
(1992)

My difficulty in the second case must have been that motoring charges, even serious ones such as these, usually permitted a grant of bail, though often with conditions. There must have considerations pointing strongly against this. I do not record these, though I added later 'I think we did right'.

The decision to refuse bail will be harder when the charge the defendant faces is unlikely to attract custody on conviction. Here is an instance:

'In a third case the problem was bail. Should a young man stay in custody when the charge was of theft of goods valued at £6? [Imprisonment is most unlikely, though available, as a sentence for theft of that order]. The original reason for custody was fear that he wouldn't turn up and his lack of 'community ties' and we concluded that this still applied. A social worker told us that the man refused all co operation, that his family had rejected him, that no one, ie no bail hostel, would take him in on grounds of his behaviour. Remand in custody maintained until Tuesday (for the case to be reviewed as I remember). He was described as not being within the scope of the Mental Health Act while suffering from 'a personality disorder'. What's the difference? He remained silent when called on to speak – evidence, I suppose, of some disorder as this was to his disadvantage. Sad.' (1991)

The day of this hearing was a Friday: what our decision meant was that this young man would suffer a further three days detention before being produced to hear the outcome of the prosecutor's review – that is, to learn whether or not the Crown was going to proceed with the matter. The three of us, in all likelihood, would never discover this. The prosecution must have seemed to those reviewing it within the Crown Prosecution Service to be an easy one to abandon: on the lowest and easiest view, the defendant would already have incurred a penalty fully up to serving as punishment – if not formally punishment – for the theft of goods worth as little as £6.

The bail decision is likely to be an uncomfortable one in cases where imprisonment on conviction will not even be an option, because the offence with which the defendant is charged is one for which custody is not available. Magistrates sometimes find themselves refusing bail in such instances, usually because there seems to be no other way of ensuring a defendant's presence.

Difficulties of a different order are found when persons accused of an offence are, for some reason, not dealt with on the same occasion:

'We had a boy of sixteen, charged with robbery, before us because his two associates, dealt with before he was arrested, were adults. [Juveniles are dealt with by the adult courts, where the charge is one of joint enterprise with adults]. He sat in front of the dock with his father, a cab-driver, other family in the gallery. Hard to be sure what the robbery amounted to – what degree of force was used – but only £5 was stolen. We should have probed this more. At the time of this supposed offence he was on bail on two other charges of attempted robbery. This fact pointed strongly against our giving him bail now. On the other hand, his two associates had both been given bail on *this* charge. Also he was sixteen and had a father who seemed concerned and, so far we could see, responsible. Also, the care of the local authority, where he'd have had to go, seemed likely to be corrupting even if secure. What would he learn there? So, by 2-1, Mrs L— [one of the bench] dissenting, we gave conditional bail. The boy responded little when I announced this, barely replying to questions. The father wept.' (1994)

This seems to have been the right decision – though we would never know whether it was right or not. It seems to have been taken not altogether for the right reason: two out of the three of us were concerned for consistency of treatment with his associates, though the associates may not have been already on bail, as he was, at the time of this latest – alleged – offence. Inconsistency of treatment may be fully justifiable where there is a relevant difference in the facts, as there seems to have been here.

Sometimes the problems are intractable:

'An awkward bail decision: the offender had had a long prison sentence, during which he'd become addicted to heroin. Released, he'd taken to petty theft to cover this indulgence. We had to sentence him on three Guilty pleas to possessing 'hard' drugs and were asked to remand him on bail for a fortnight before doing this, so that he could undertake 'drying-out', i.e. anti-addiction therapy at an establishment I'd never heard of. The problem was that this so-called therapy plan rested on his mere assertion; his advocate described efforts to get from the place evidence that it might be viable – but to no avail in the time. Beyond this was the likelihood of re-offending. He'd been sentenced for shoplifting on Tuesday (offence committed on bail), given a conditional discharge, and then re-offended almost at once. On this ground we refused bail, remanded him in custody and called for a pre-sentence report [from the probation service]. I think this was inevitable, but the fact was we've sent back to prison a man with this dreadful addiction and thereby, perhaps, impeded his cure.'

I concluded with words which might have served to wind up many such records:

> 'Came away with a sense of whom it is – often – we deal with: the wounded and embittered and inadequate, those whom some weakness has pretty well ruined. My sense of a shared human nature is very sobering.' (1998)

Either side has the right of appeal to the Crown Court from the decision of magistrates on a bail application. This is as it should be, and magistrates who have ended the day in some doubt over what they decided will be glad of it. I recall one such case, where I was in the chair:

> ' ... a bail application from a man charged with theft and burglary. The oddity is that the supposed victim is his son's girlfriend; his wife and his son are lined up to be prosecution witnesses. The prosecution case on the burglary charge seems to us weak. We think the risk of further offending on bail to be negligible, and so resolve to grant bail on conditions, one of which is to live and sleep at home (no obvious alternative place of residence). When I announce these conditions, there's an immediate strong demur from the prosecutrix, which we should have anticipated. The wife is said to have visited him in prison and is said to be reconciled. We now concede that this should be checked, and it is, and is confirmed. The prosecutrix continues to express concern over his enforced proximity to prosecution witnesses. I said that the ordinary sanctions of the law will apply [against the intimidation of witnesses]. We leave it at that, and remind the prosecutrix that she can appeal.'

On this occasion there was no immediate notice of appeal, which would have had the effect of blocking the release of the defendant. Whether or not there was an appeal I never discovered. The likelihood of the charges being dropped must have been high, given the wife's presumed unwillingness to testify. That would have seemed a further reason for giving bail. Nonetheless, I was discontented with myself:

> 'This wasn't well handled. We should have gone in and said we were *minded* to impose the residence condition and then taken it from there. We'd have been very awkwardly placed if it had turned out that the wife objected to his presence.' (2006)

I came to believe, over my twenty years on the bench, that there was one respect in which magistrates were in part responsible for the problems and irritations brought about by the bailing of defendants. Here, I do not have in mind misjudgements on their part, in dealing with applications, of which I have just given an example. Some misjudgements will be inevitable. The point is the simpler one that the requirement placed on defendants receiving bail to present themselves at court on the specified day, and in proper time, is not made sufficiently rigorous. Default is for much of the time treated as a relatively minor matter, rarely attracting the short spell of imprisonment which is within the court's powers. If magistrates give the impression that arriving late, or forgetting to arrive at all, matters not all that much, it is unsurprising that that view of the matter has become the standard one in the world outside. Failure to answer to bail is a criminal offence, resulting in an obvious social cost, notably the waste of court-time and the placing of an avoidable burden on the police.

So much for bail. The signing by judges or magistrates of warrants, authorising, or positively requiring, the police or some other public authority to take draconian action raises many of the same questions. In each case there is a sharp interference with someone's liberty or normal rights, such as the right to sit in peace at home without disruption. In each case, an effectively administrative decision is taken by a judicial authority, which has to keep in mind, in so doing, fairness and due proportion. A difference is that, in issuing warrants there is no need, as there is in the case of bail, to hear both sides. Indeed, the action that follows the issue of a warrant will have surprise of its essence.

The role of magistrates in issuing warrants is much more restricted than it was. The powers of the police to arrest supposed offenders for questioning are laid down in statute and magistrates become involved only when the prosecuting authorities wish to detain someone for more than the brief period specified. The warrants which I was regularly invited to sign were different. Usually they were authorisations to the police to search premises for the evidence of criminal activity. The application was usually made in court, in an interval between other items of business, and by a police officer in plain clothes. The officer takes the oath, or makes affirmation, and swears to the truth of what is asserted in a document laid before the bench. If one is persuaded of this, at least in broad outline, there are unlikely to be obvious grounds for refusing the application, but questions may be asked and assurances sought. The planned entry may be forced and may well be in the early morning. In such a case, it will be worth checking if the police know if young children are likely to be on the premises and, if so, how they plan to minimise the effect on them of an unexpected and noisy bursting-in of strange men. Most commonly, at least on my own bench, the application was to enter premises thought to be used for the supply of illegal drugs. These were unlikely to contain children – or so we were commonly assured. The question remains worth asking.

The other main category of application was for the warrants required for action under the Mental Health Act 1983. The difficulties here were quite different. There would rarely be any suspicion of criminality. The application would be made by the local authority, in conjunction with a doctor. It would be to enter premises occupied by someone known to be mentally ill or whose behaviour suggested acute mental illness. Very often it was complaints by the neighbours, usually about noise or verbal abuse, which had brought the problem to attention. The information presented to the bench would often suggest that there was a risk of suicide, less commonly a risk of harm to others. Here too, the case for firm and urgent intervention seemed quite clear, and a warrant would be required to authorise it. The questions I was inclined to put to the applicant, who would be a local authority social worker, were not prompted by any real doubt on the main point. I usually asked whether or not the object of the process was known to have any family and, if so, whether its members were aware of what was happening. The answer was usually 'yes' to both. There was no question of family-members being present during the application, but I was conscious that they might have an interest, to say the least. A front door would in all likelihood be broken down. Whose job would it be to make the premises secure? At whose cost would it be? Could this be done effectively? Would they be told where their relative was to be detained?

Both police and social workers usually dealt reassuringly with questions such as these. I was sometimes reminded, when they did so, of the answers served up to a fairly predictable set of examination questions. There was a sense of rehearsal and prepared delivery. The value of the procedure must have lain largely its ensuring that some of the more obvious wider consequences of what was in contemplation had had some consideration. I had little sense that I, or any magistrate, would ever be able to form a worthwhile independent view of the merits of what was proposed.

Applications for warrants were not always made in court; sometimes they were judged by the applicants to be so urgent that they had to be made to a magistrate 'out of hours' – that is, during the evening, sometimes in the middle of the night. This procedure may have been inescapable, but it could be hazardous. Applications presented while the court is sitting would have been passed up through a legal advisor who would have made some obvious checks, such as seeing that the statute under which it is proposed to act was the one which was applicable. Once the warrant was signed, the paperwork which had accompanied it could be filed away at the court. Applications 'out of hours' had to be handled without this useful back-up, though advice from legal advisors should have been obtainable over the telephone. There remained a greater risk of error in the taking of what should always be regarded as a serious decision, the invasion of someone's home and, with Mental Health Act warrants, his or her probable enforced removal.

The procedure just described is, no doubt, still found, though in the case of my own former bench it has been modified. I return to that in Chapter Ten. In my time on the bench, the police and the social workers with applications to make would usually contact the magistrate they meant to approach over the telephone. This was to confirm that he or she would be at home and sufficiently at leisure to deal with the matter. It also gave the magistrate the chance to make some preliminary inquiries which might have aborted the application or led to its being deferred. It was my own practice to do this with applications for search warrants, and I sometimes concluded from the policeman's answers that an investigation which might have been in hand for ten days or more had reached a point at six o'clock in the evening when a search warrant seemed to be required. On such occasions, I usually concluded that there was no good reason why the application should not stand over until the morning and be presented at court. I therefore declined to sign. The policeman's reaction suggested that this was an unusual outcome.

Mental Health Act applications were a different case: there was rarely any doubt about their urgency. What was of prime importance was to check that the proper procedure had been followed. It is a requirement of the Act that the application should come from an 'approved' social worker – to ensure that it is made by someone with the right training and expertise – and the 'approval' is subject to periodical renewal. On one occasion, when I asked to see the document recording 'approval', I found that this had lapsed some ten days earlier. The applicant told me that this was attributable to bureaucratic incompetence; he would certainly have been 'approved' if the local authority managed its business better. I thought this was very probably the case. Nonetheless, if I had signed the warrant, the action which would have followed, which I would have authorised, would have been unlawful. I refused to sign it, but with much moral discomfort, as the information that accompanied it was to the effect that a vulnerable individual was in a very bad way. I was left to trust that the application would be renewed and, at second attempt, made by someone properly entitled to make it.

I had come close to making one of the worst mistakes possible for a magistrate, acting outside my powers. Readers of Pepys' diary may recall that the diarist, who was a justice of the peace by virtue of his office as Clerk of the Acts at the Navy Board, once made this mistake. In 1662, a man called Field sued him for wrongful arrest and obtained £30 in damages. In the case I have just described, it is unlikely in the extreme that I would have been sued and, if damages had been awarded against me and, no doubt, against the social worker, the cries of indignation from the magistracy at large would have been loud. This reaction, observable from time to time, should make defenders of the lay magistracy uncomfortable. A magistrate should be ready to accept full responsibility, extending to responsibility for blunders.

Whenever I refused an application for a warrant 'out of hours', I was aware that the applicant could pick up the phone and repeat the application to another justice, who might have been more accommodating. This would of course be quite improper, but in all probability it would have been undetected. How often, I wonder, does it happen? It would certainly be unsurprising if police officers and other applicants prefer to approach magistrates who need little or no persuasion to sign. In twenty years on the bench, I was only very infrequently contacted at home. The main reason for this must have been that I lived further away from our two courthouses than many of my colleagues, who were the first recourse for police officers wanting a signature. I came to suspect however that I was approached even less often than this fact alone would have determined and to attribute this to my practice of quite often refusing applications, usually because those for search warrants lacked any real urgency. Here I can only speculate, but it seems likely that any magistrate seen to be 'difficult' will be left alone. The implications of all this hardly flatter the lay magistracy.

7.

Is it Efficient?

The Inefficiencies of the System

Our observer from the gallery, if he had been persistent in his attendance, would in all likelihood have seen much that would have struck him as odd and inefficient. His friend from the continent, to whom the adversarial process would probably have been a novelty, might have been impressed yet more unfavourably. Previous chapters will have exposed much to substantiate such reactions. The present Justice Secretary's outburst is fully comprehensible. In my early years on the bench, I often walked away from a day in court feeling exasperated, although I realised that much of what had not gone well may well have been no one's fault, or at least not obviously so. Hearings often have to be adjourned, if nearly always for reasons which are easy to appreciate. Very often it is on account of the absence of a witness who, it is claimed, is needed if a trial is to be fair. This default will often have been the needed witness' fault, but it may have been because he was ill or had some other good reason for being elsewhere. It is up to the court to probe these excuses, and in the early days of my service on the bench it often seemed to me that my more experienced colleagues were too little rigorous in doing so. An appreciation of witnesses' problems is only right but too much of it may inconvenience other witnesses who have presented themselves on the day set down, often not for the first time:

'One trial set down for the morning: drunk in charge of a car, the defence being that there was no likelihood of the defendant driving during the period of drunken-ness. This would have required expert evidence on each side, which was not ready. Therefore a joint application for an adjournment. We grant this with reluctance and after discussion: the trouble was that *nine* lay witnesses had attended in vain and not for the first time. I called them in and expressed regret. We thought we had to rule out taking just their evidence today, as the period of adjournment was going to be such as to make this evidence no longer fresh and 'sharp'. (1996)

The point was that if the bench had started the trial and begun taking evidence, as magistrates are often urged to do, the same three persons would have had to re-assemble at a later date to take the expert evidence. This would not have been easy to arrange, and it might have been five or six weeks before the hearing resumed. Adjournment was therefore sensible, but the burden on the lay witnesses was considerable. It would have been unsurprising if some of the nine dropped out, galled by the waste of time in two or more futile attendances. As the bench chairman of the moment, I could only apologise.

An application to adjourn the hearing may come from either side and it is open to the other side to oppose it. Applications from the prosecution are most often on the ground that a witness, often a police officer, is unavoidably absent. This is often because the officer is on leave, the date having been booked for leave months in advance. The applicant usually admits that the prosecutor on the previous occasion, when the trial date was settled, had not been informed of this. Here is an instance of inefficiency for which there is no real excuse and which is all too common.

If the court refuses the application and tells the prosecutor to go ahead, he or she will proceed and make the best of a bad job or, much more probably, offer no evidence, leaving the court no option but to dismiss the charge. The court will take its decision on the application after inviting the defendant or his legal representative to react, using some such form of words as: 'The prosecutor has asked for an adjournment; do you oppose this application?' If there is a legal representative, he will almost always oppose it, knowing that if he gets his way he will probably – and after a fashion – win his case by default. An unrepresented defendant may not appreciate how much he stands to gain by opposing the application. In such a case, I often wondered if he should be prompted to do so by the bench. The bench must not take sides, but it may seem right to minimise the disadvantages to a naive defendant of being unrepresented, and to drop a broad hint.

Some defendants show themselves well aware of what they need to do:

> '... taking a vehicle without consent and driving without insurance – defendant aged seventeen and looking younger. He asserted that he wanted no legal advice and opposed the prosecutor's request for an adjournment (no witnesses) – smart this, of course. We refused the request and then dismissed the case.' (1991)

On this occasion, I found in myself a degree of sympathy for the defendant. I had heard nothing of the facts which the prosecutor would have sought to establish but I saw someone up against a formidable machine who, but for our decision, would have suffered a disagreeable suspense even longer. This, it struck me, would have been oppressive. To the words already quoted, I added: 'Nice to see this *naif*-seeming youth walking away whistling, as it were'. I doubt if I would feel that now, but I have no doubt that our decision to refuse the request for an adjournment was right, as it is only by taking such a line regularly that the courts are able to exert pressure on prosecutors to be efficient. The price to be paid for this, a considerable one, is that the victims of crime are likely to feel that justice has been denied them.

Not all delays brought about by incompetence are attributable to the prosecution. Sometimes a defence solicitor's conduct of a case will have been incompetent. He or she may have failed to meet some procedural requirement or have mistaken the time or day and failed to appear in court when it was necessary. Quite often, the staff of the court will be found to have failed to take some necessary step, such as informing a defendant of an adjournment date. Here, magistrates can do little more than ask their clerk to try to identify the person at fault and pass on a reprimand. Anyone who has worked in a large organisation will know how hard it is to attribute specific defaults to individuals, certainly when weeks have elapsed. Some lapses on the part of clerical staff have drastic consequences. It often happens that a defendant has been charged with several offences, pleading Guilty at an early stage to some of them but not to all. At his trial on those that remain it is important and strictly required that the magistrates, or the jury in the case of a trial in the Crown Court, should be kept in ignorance of the Guilty pleas so that their approach to the disputed charges before them is unprejudiced. Occasionally this requirement is ignored and the charges where the defendant has pleaded Guilty appear on the register with an indication of that plea. What follows when this is realised is likely to perplex our supposed observer in the gallery:

'... we prepare to try a man on charges of having a bladed instrument and of having a small quantity of cannabis. It at once becomes clear that the latter has been listed in error as he's already indicated a Guilty plea. The question then arises whether we should disqualify ourselves from trying the former. The legal representative of the defendant indicates 'no objection' to our trying it; the clerk (to my irritation) advises that we should see if another court can take the case. My colleagues – I'm in the chair – want to take this advice, so we retire.'

This absence from the courtroom gave the defendant and his advisor a chance to confer and they must have taken it:

'When we return we get a Guilty plea on *both* cases, so proceed to sentence.' (1993)

This change of plea on the bladed instrument charge saved everyone the trouble of trying to find another tribunal. This might have proved impracticable, in which case the matter would have had to be adjourned to another date, perhaps weeks ahead. This would have extended the strain on the defendant and brought about extra cost. What I will call 'legitimate inefficiency' would have required it, though only the incompetence of a clerk in the back office made it necessary.

It is as important that magistrates starting a trial should know nothing of any previous convictions the defendant may have as that they should be unaware of his present admissions. The point is the same, that there should be nothing to prejudice them. Unawareness by the support staff of a Crown Court of the importance of this resulted, on one occasion, in my being given a list of an appellant's 'previous' in the folder of papers I was handed on arrival. The other magistrate and the judge were in the same plight:

'... a manifest lapse on the part of the staff of the court. It would have meant we'd have had to disqualify ourselves and adjourn [the appeal].

As it happened, this point was never reached:

> '... before this point was raised, there was another submission, that we should find that there was an abuse of process in the Crown's continuing with the case. One plank in this was that of the three policemen called to the scene of the supposed assault two were 'lost', i.e. no one was sure who they were or whether they were still serving and the third was appearing for the defence, and that no adequate record of the complaint seemed to have been taken. Another was that through a succession of mischances the appeal had already been adjourned several times. Another was that a piece of evidence – the supposed victim's shirt – had been left to be stored at the court after the last listing of the case and now couldn't be found. I wasn't persuaded this was an abuse of process – though it seemed that some of it would be good grounds for squashing the conviction if and when the appeal was heard. But I was voted down on this.'

This meant that, through the incompetence of the police and the prosecution together, and not on its merits, though, had it been put to us, it may have seemed to have merits, the appeal would succeed. That did not have to be the end of the matter:

> 'I then proposed that we should announce that we were considering a bind-over. The judge seemed against this, then to my surprise made just that announcement. A strong plea from the appellant's counsel persuaded us to drop the idea [of binding over the appellant]. We then gave the appellant costs. So he won all along the line, though he showed little satisfaction ...' (1997)

The only satisfaction we ourselves could find at the end of this long run of incompetence was in the reaching of that end: my two colleagues were probably right in calling a halt, after an appreciable charge to public funds and – possibly – the failure to obtain justice for the alleged victim. It is unlikely that anyone was called to account for what went wrong.

The Exploitation of Procedure

Distinct from the plain incompetence shown on occasions such as these is the exploitation of procedure by defence advocates. This may take several forms. One of the commonest grounds for adjourning hearings is the failure of the prosecution (the CPS or the police) to supply the defence with copies of documents or other material of which the prosecutor will make use at the forthcoming trial. Typically, these are the record of a police-station interview with the defendant, witness-statements on which the prosecutor will rely and, perhaps, the closed-circuit-television (CCTV) record. If the CPS and the police were better at handing over in good time everything that the defence is entitled to see, there would be much less scope for the defence to apply for adjournments. As it is, it will be tempting for defence advocates to ask for more material than they need in the expectation – and hope – of not getting it. Where the defence case is weak, and conviction at trial very likely, the appeal of acting so as to string things out will be obvious. If matters are strung out enough and indispensable witnesses tire of attending court to no purpose, there will be a chance that the prosecution will be dropped. Another stratagem is to ask the prosecution to present as witnesses more police officers that the prosecution itself finds to be necessary. The justification advanced is likely to be that a certain officer, or more than one, needs to be available for cross-examination even if the prosecution does not need him or them for evidence-in- chief. The more police officers are picked out to appear, the greater the likelihood of one or more of them being absent on the day of trial. Here again, there will be arguable grounds for an adjournment. And so it goes on.

It is difficult for magistrates to estimate how often such tactics are employed, as they may have little idea, at this early stage in the progress of a case, of the cogency of the anticipated defence. It is where the defence will be weak, and where the defence advocate knows it, that there may be recourse to desperate measures. It is hard to condemn this recourse, as in the case of documents and a CCTV record there is likely to be a plain entitlement. I will therefore say only that we have procedures which seem open to tactical exploitation, even though nothing is done which offends against a solicitor's or counsel's professional code.

Legitimate Inefficiency

By legitimate inefficiency I mean rules, precedents and points of procedure which offend against a 'businesslike' standard of efficiency but which are nonetheless required by a proper judicial standard – in a word, by fairness. These are of all kinds. Very early in my service, a couple from the continent, apparently tourists, appeared charged with theft. This is a so-called 'either-way' offence, and those charged have the right to choose to be tried before a judge and jury in the Crown Court. This was explained to them and, through their interpreter, they exercised this right. The value of the goods said to have been stolen, two cans of a soft drink, was £1.50. We adjourned the hearing for the matter to be transferred to the Crown Court and bailed the defendants to appear there. Did they do so? I never found out, but it must have been unlikely. They can hardly have feared extradition proceedings. If they did skip bail, they would have saved the public the cost of their trial before a judge and jury, involving an interpreter certainly and legal representation quite possibly.

The cost of proceeding, against these defendants, even before magistrates, was out of all proportion to the value of the goods allegedly stolen; before the Crown Court, if they did after all present themselves there, the disproportion would have been greater still. Here is a kind of inefficiency. It is a kind which can be minimised, and which often is, by making it common practice not to prosecute where the offence seems trivial. It is hard to say that the police should have taken that view here, even if few people would have blamed them if they had. How can petty theft be ignored simply on account of its pettiness? Why should retailers be denied the normal protection of the law and left to put up with pilfering? There will often be considerations distinct from calculations of cost, which have to be over-riding.

Sometimes the incompetence of prosecutors leads to something essential being overlooked. Once this has become apparent, there may be an application to resume the presentation of a case which has been formally closed:

'... case of assaulting a police officer – defendant a large Nigerian man charged with swinging a punch on being pushed into a cell. The prosecutor didn't seem incompetent – though he had to concede that a statement of medical evidence had been sent to the defence too late to be admissible. It was therefore a surprise when, when he'd closed his case, defence counsel argued that a vital piece of evidence had been left out – there'd been no proof that the man was properly in custody, and therefore no evidence that the PC was 'on duty' with regard to him. After much argument we accepted this   no case to answer. [That is, we dismissed the charge]. I think this was right, but had much sympathy for the probably assaulted policeman. The evidence that should have been put in [to establish that he was properly in custody] was available in court, but we refused to allow re-opening.' (1991)

Another application to re-open the prosecution case came up when a bus driver was charged with endangering a passenger, after a comparable lapse from the prosecutor:

'... the trial of a bus driver for shutting his door on an alighting passenger, an elderly woman, with the consequence that she falls into the gutter – eloquent in evidence on her feelings as she lay there, contemplating a wheel start to revolve forwards. We heard the Crown's case, which seemed strong – evidence of the fallen woman and of an eyewitness. 'That is the case for the prosecution, your worships.' We are then surprised by a submission [from the defence] of no-case-to-answer: there had been no evidence that the man on trial had been the driver. At this, the CPS solicitor wants to re-open his case – he had a policeman outside who had come just to establish that – entirely his own fault that he'd overlooked the point. On the 're-opening' point we take advice and hear submissions on both sides – it seems clear that there's no adequate ground to let him re-open. So we dismiss the charge. The victim and her eyewitness both look sick, and I'm not surprised.' (1993)

The advice we took was from the clerk and it was grounded in decisions of the higher courts. It seemed plain from these decisions that a case may be reopened and fresh evidence put to the court only with a view to meeting a technical requirement, of the kind unlikely to be contentious. We concluded with little debate that evidence of identity could not be presented as merely technical. With more experience and some reflection, I have little doubt that this was right. For the victim, however, the outcome may have been more than merely disappointing. It may have threatened to weaken the force of any claim for damages she may have had it in mind to pursue.

'Common Sense' and 'Natural Justice'

The fiasco, as it certainly was, which I have just described, brings out the difference between two sorts of intuitive judgment, those of common sense and those bearing on natural justice. Common sense would say that when there was a policeman who had attended to give evidence, as there was on that occasion, that policeman should have been heard, and that a lapse on the part of the prosecutor need not be a block to that. Common sense would go to say that to decline to hear him amounted to a denial of justice to the woman who had suffered the accident and that every consideration of social utility, notably that of deterrence, pointed to our proceeding with the trial. The claims of common sense are commonly taken to be over-riding, so much so that only philosophers are brazen enough to repudiate them.

The cry for 'common sense' is often voiced in the media and by politicians, usually going well beyond criticism of particular decisions such as these, where they may indeed be telling. In July 2010 a prominent Labour backbencher, Mr Austin Mitchell, wrote, in a letter to *The Times*:

> ' ... Clarke can uphold the principle of deterrence as well as closing swathes of magistrates' courts, but only if there is an end to the amateurish game-playing culture that prevails throughout the system...'

There is a real point here, and the complaint about 'game-playing' has been voiced also by the higher judiciary. The term is highly resonant, but people understand it differently. Among other things, Mitchell probably means something which I have just considered, the duplication of witnesses to no purpose or the bids for adjournments for no real cause. He – and others – may however mean the well-timed submission of 'no case', made by a lawyer who is properly alert, of which I have just recorded instances. That is not open to the same objection. It may well be the case that on the evidence the prosecutor has presented there is no case for the defendant to answer. If there is not, it must be right to say so. Mitchell, indeed, has a broader target in view:

> 'Backward inefficient adversarial legal systems achieve only low conviction rates and have to compensate for this by punishing excessively severely. Inquisitorial systems can punish more leniently because there is much greater certainty of punishment.'

Here is the voice of a kind of bluff common sense which, to all intents and purposes, thinks that the guilt of those charged, or of almost all of them, can simply be assumed. A conviction rate is then seen to be something 'achieved'. A low conviction rate is seen as tantamount to failure.

At this point, faced with such presumptions, I can say only that notions of natural justice point the other way. These notions are held intuitively and almost universally. The cry, 'It isn't fair,' is as widely made as the appeal to common sense. Those who raise that cry may well not be of one mind over what constitutes fairness. In particular, there may be disagreement over what natural justice requires when criminal procedure is in question. For all that, few people would deny that a basic requirement is that there should be no presumption of the guilt of the person charged on the part of the tribunal. Mitchell seems to make just this presumption and would, I think, find few supporters. Most people would say also that one component of any fair procedure is that the prosecution should open and state its case and then draw a firm line when it has done so. It seems to be a breach of natural justice to give the prosecution a second chance to put in evidence after it has drawn that line, and possibly after the defence has begun to respond.

Here is a clash of intuitions. It is well outside the scope of the present work to try to resolve it in general and in principle. In my time on the bench I felt little need to attempt this resolution. On each of the two occasions to which I have just referred it was as clear to the two colleagues sitting with me as it was to me that it was natural justice which had to be decisive, at least when what had to be decided was the admissibility of evidence and the broader conduct of a trial. The judicial guidance that was quoted to us seemed to be in a welcome harmony with these intuitions. Both occasions came quite early in my time on the bench and, together, they left me sharply aware that the doing of justice cannot be a matter of common sense alone and that much that would count as inefficient on that criterion has to be accepted. Otherwise put, the doing of justice comes at a price, in part financial, but not wholly so. Plainly as I recognised this, I was quite as clear that in many ways the system in which I was serving worked badly, and that this was not attributable to the over-riding importance of justice. There were weaknesses both in the machinery of justice and in the performance of individuals, which often wasted public money and bore hard on vulnerable people.

The Drive to Improve Things

I have given the date of all the quotations from my diaries to be found above, which can be seen to come from the earlier part of my time on the bench. I should now record – and emphasise – that I observed some improvement across the range after about 1995, notably in the performance in court of CPS prosecutors. Where the efficiency of the doing of summary justice did not improve, there was at least an increasingly widely held sense that it needed to. With the new century, it became apparent that this sense had spread into Whitehall. In 2002 there was a White Paper and in 2003 a new enactment, the Criminal Justice Act of 2003. A contemporary commentator recorded this development. He wrote:

> 'The Government's latest criminal justice bill, due to become law this autumn, marks a new departure in criminal justice reform. For several decades now, nearly all judicial reforms have sought to ensure that no innocent person ever faces a guilty verdict. Now this new bill sets out "to rebalance the criminal justice system in favour of the victim and the community". This mantra reoccurs throughout last year's 159-page white paper that preceded the bill, along with observations such as: "a criminal trial is not a game under which a guilty defendant should be provided with a sporting chance".'

This was how the playwright, Jonathan Myerson, opened a long article, *The Justice Gap: A Magistrate's Tale*, in the magazine *Prospect* (June 2003). I am obliged to *Prospect* for permission to quote from this, the whole of which is well worth reading. In 2003 Myerson was a Youth Court magistrate in Inner London, and it was on the basis of his experience in that role that he offered a warm endorsement of the new direction announced in the White Paper. The new direction was most conspicuous in the form of changes to the criminal law and procedure, which applied to magistrates' courts but which were probably of much more significance to the Crown Court. There were steps to make magistrates aware of these changes which became part of the repertoire of the clerks in their routine briefing of members of the bench in court. Myerson welcomes them, at the same time as he describes, at length and with evident feeling, the regular frustration and irritation brought about by incompetence and by the exploitation of tactical advantage. Here there is more of a problem, as the procedures of which advantage may be taken at least will have been established on account of the need to be fair to defendants. As for the mere incompetence, all that Myerson records might have come from the record of my own experience, on which I have just drawn.

What makes this article memorable is however the account to which he proceeds, which is of the process which followed the mugging of his twelve-year-old son in July 2001. Myerson was directly involved as a father in a sequence of events which he was well qualified to appraise as a Youth Court magistrate. He sums up what happened:

> '... we went to the police station to give a statement. That's when our odyssey into the victim's side of the justice system began. Thirty-nine hours later (spread over nine months) a verdict was reached. This is how Jacob and I passed that equivalent of a working week: initial statement to police on evening of incident, four hours; first ID parade, four hours; second ID parade, three and three-quarter hours; first (aborted) robbery trial, three and three-quarter hours; additional statement on witness intimidation, two and a half hours; second robbery trial, eight hours; extra witness intimidation statement, two hours; first (aborted) witness intimidation trial, four hours 15 minutes; second witness intimidation trial, six hours and three-quarters. Total spent on a minor matter of justice: 39 hours.

> 'In fact, you can double this to 78 victim-hours because I had to accompany Jacob through every stage of the process...'

A major complication here was an attempt to intimidate the victim, Myerson's son, leading, as we see, to a further charge. It will be seen that, even without this, the burden on the victim and his family would have been heavy. It is no wonder that many defendants give up.

As a magistrate, I came to have my own perspective on many more than one such 'odyssey', at the time of their listing for trial. When the back-history of a matter before us seemed to have been complicated, it was common to ask the clerk to spell it out for us. We quite often got much the same picture, not indeed from the point of view of a prosecution witness but making that point of view easily imaginable. Many more such cases will never have come to a court's direct attention, but will simply have been abandoned.

A revision of the Criminal Procedure Rules (CPR) was issued in 2005, to strong effect. Here was an attempt, coming with high judicial authority, to speed up criminal process and make it more efficient. This was so obviously necessary that it was widely welcomed, as I recall, by the members of my bench, who came together, along with their legal advisors, to study what was prescribed. From one angle, that contained little that was surprising. The detailed prescriptions of the Rules were presented as lying within the inherent power of a court of law to settle its procedure and manage its business efficiently. The Rules set out the duty of both the court and of the participants in the process – for this purpose anyone involved in any way with a criminal case. The duty of the court itself is to further the overriding objective of doing justice by actively managing the case that has been put before it. Here the word that matters is 'actively'. The court's duty is found to include the early identification of the real issues and of the needs of witnesses, setting timetables, giving directions on the serving of documents on the other side, and monitoring the progress of the case and compliance with directions.

In 2007 (in the case of Narinder Malcolm v DPP) the High Court declared, in words that are worth quoting, that:

> 'criminal trials are no longer to be treated as a game, in which any move is final, and any omissions by the prosecution leads

to its failure. It is the duty of the defence to make its defence and the issues it raises clear to the prosecution and to the court at an early stage. The duty is implicit in r 3.3 of the CPR, which requires the parties actively to assist the exercise by the courts of its case management powers, the exercise of which requires early identification of the real issues.'

Here is another reference to the need to break with the treatment of legal process as a game; this rather dangerous analogy, as I take it to be, must be appealing, or it would not be found so often.

In the case of my own bench, doing what was now required – or, rather, what had always been required, if not done – brought about a slight modification of routine. After the reissue of the CPR, it became normal practice for the three magistrates forming a bench to confer with their clerk, before going into court, and to review their list with the object of picking out what would require case-management. We would then receive the clerk's advice on what seemed to be necessary. The clerk would come into this meeting with the court file on the case and would brief the bench on the outcome of previous hearings and on whether there had been orders by the court. This adjustment of routine could only be helpful to justices with an extended role, which was not an easy one, and it appears to have become common practice. There must be a question, however, if it is fully compatible with fairness to defendants. If the clerk's briefings are not to be in open court, is there not a risk of something of a 'steer' being given, to which a defence advocate, if made aware of it, would have wished to object? In the more delicate case of the unrepresented defendant, likely to know nothing of legal procedure, how should he be supposed to react to having the progression of his case discussed in his absence, before he will have been in any position to speak for himself?

He will almost certainly be unaware of the probability of this happening, something which seems to raise further doubts as to its propriety.

As for adjournments, there is now a regular call, both from the higher courts and from ministers concerned with the cost of legal proceedings, for magistrates to break with what is sometimes called 'the adjournment culture'. Effective case-management should do much to lessen the need for adjournment. There are now checklists for the use of magistrates who will be faced with applications to adjourn, clear, consisting of the numerous questions which might usefully be put to applicants before a decision is taken. It is however quite unrealistic to expect that even unfailingly good case-management will end the need to adjourn. In one recent case, publicised only because of the defendant's celebrity, some inescapable difficulties stand out. In November 2010, Paul Gascoigne, the footballer, and another man appeared before Northallerton Magistrates' Court. For what follows I depend on the report in *The Times*.

Gascoigne's solicitor asked for an adjournment on the grounds that he had received the papers in the case only two days previously and had met his client only that morning. This was refused, and the solicitor then withdrew from the case on the grounds that he would be in no position to do his duty by his client. Gascoigne was told that he would have to conduct his own defence. The other defendant's solicitor then asked for an adjournment on the grounds, to quote the press report, 'that his client's case could potentially be prejudiced by the way that Mr Gascoigne would conduct his own defence'. The bench refused this application also. These two submissions and their consideration appear to have used up the morning. 'At 1.45pm everyone was back in place – for a discussion about whether there was enough time left in the day for the trial to be heard.

The magistrates retired again...' There decision, announced on their return was that the case would not proceed that day. A new date was fixed, some five weeks in the future. It can be assumed that the defendants would have been bailed to appear then.

The tone of the report in *The Times* is jocular, but the observer from the gallery would be likely to see the outcome as scandalous rather than laughable. The original time-estimate for the trial of the two defendants was probably a whole day. The magistrates' decision not to start after the lunch-break was therefore quite understandable: they would have been unlikely to finish the trial before a reasonable stopping-time, in particular because the trial of an unrepresented defendant will take longer. It should however have been possible to have made a start, perhaps in the hope of hearing at least the whole of the prosecution case, and to have adjourned after making at least that much progress. Magistrates are often exhorted to do this, and the bench probably considered doing so here. The objection to doing so is that it is usually difficult to find an early date at which it will be possible for three magistrates, two solicitors and two defendants to re-assemble. A further objection is that on re-assembling, perhaps after some weeks, the magistrates would have heard the defence case – on this occasion, the cases of two defendants – when much of the detail and sharpness of the prosecution case would have been lost.

What happened on one day at Northallerton brings persistent difficulties into sharp relief. The bench's 'robust' decision to refuse two applications to adjourn suggests that they had absorbed and were acting on exhortations to break with the 'adjournment culture'. What brings in a touch of farce is that the making and then the consideration of the applications took so long that they had to adjourn anyway. The jocularity of the press report is understandable. A district judge, sitting solo, would not have needed to retire, as there would have no need to consult. Does what happened here suggest that district judges should take over cases like this, or all cases? The briskness of a one-person tribunal has its own limitations. May it not be preferable to have three people go out to talk through what has been put to them? For a further consideration of these points, see the closing chapter of this book.

HOW IT CAME ABOUT

8.

How it Started

Quarter Sessions

This book now becomes a work of history, though only briefly. This chapter and the next may be skipped by those with no interest in history – though, I believe, at their loss. Some awareness of the history of the magistracy is needed for a full understanding of how things are now and for a sound calculation of how they might be.

An Act of 1361, in the reign of Edward III, provided for the appointment by the king of certain office-holders and of others, at the king's choice, to what were styled Commissions of the Peace, one for each English county and for each large town which was treated as a county. This was probably no more than a formalisation of arrangements alrady in place, giving them the authority of statute Those appointed – the so-called Justices of the Peace – were to meet quarterly and empowered to call before them anyone judged to have breached the king's peace or to be threatening to do so and to take sureties for their good behaviour. In this, we can make out the origin of the court of Quarter Sessions, as it came to be known, not at this point quite a court, as we now understand it. It was to become one as responsibilities came to be assigned to it which gave it that character.

The Commission of the Peace became a prime element in the government of England in the fifteenth and later centuries. The speed of the devplment is striking, as is the range and complexity of the magistracy's functions in the early modern period and beyond. These extended from the day-to-day administration of those parts of the country for which each commission was responsible, now the role of local authorities, to the enforcement of law-and-order, now the role of the police, to conducting trials, along with a jury, and passing sentence on those convicted. This last was the one role which Quarter Sessions retained to the end, and exercised alongside Assize courts.

The eighteenth century and the first three quarters of the nineteenth were the heyday of the county magistrates. Membership of a county commission was an essential mark of status and those appointed tended to serve on it all their lives. There was a property qualification and those who delivered justice, at least in the county commissions, must have been so much richer than those who received it as to be almost always outside the range of bribery. They must also have been too secure in their position and authority to be at any risk of intimidation.

Active membership of a county commission was often left to a small group of the relatively young, made up of the few prepared to shoulder not only the quarterly duty of attending Sessions but also the implementation of the administrative decisions taken there. These were very few, by modern standards, but there was an irreducible minimum of local government which might need to be funded by the rates, which it was for Quarter Sessions to levy as required.

How well did the justices know the law? The original intention was that each commission was to contain at least some members who were legally qualified, in the expectation, no doubt, that points of law would in practice be left to them or they would enlighten the remainder. The commission was not to act in the absence of at least some members of this inner ring, known as the *quorum*. This was imperfectly realised. From the late sixteenth century the deficiency would have been made up, at least in part, by the practice of the sons of landowning families proceeding to the Inns of Court after a spell at a university. At least part of the object of this must have been to equip them for the judicial role they would be expected to acquire.

The appointment of magistrates lay with the Lord Chancellor, acting on behalf of the Crown, usually in close association with the Lord Lieutenant of the county in his capacity as *custos rotulorum* (the keeper of the rolls). This office,was much older than the Lieutenancy and usually held in conjunction with it. In effect, it denoted the headship of the county magistrates. The way things were done in the mid-nineteenth century is brought out by an incident in the career of Benjamin Disraeli, Conservative leader in the Commons and later Prime Minister. In 1851 Disraeli recorded that he had hoped to have his younger brother, James, appointed to the Buckinghamshire county bench and had approached the Lord Lieutenant with that object. At that time, James had been a farmer and the Lord Lieutenant had refused to consider him. Farming, as distinct from landownership, counted, at least to this Lord Lieutenant, as being in trade. Farmers got their hands dirty. If farmers were to be let in, how could businessmen be kept out? Even the doing of a favour to James' elder brother counted for too little to trump this consideration.

We glimpse a rather different kind of preference – or prejudice – in a work of fiction, in chapter eleven of Trollope's novel, *Ralph The Heir*. A landowner has two sons, the elder in all respects a better man than the younger who will, nonetheless, inherit, as the elder was born out of wedlock. We are told of the elder, 'a point had been stretched in his favour and he was a magistrate'. Here are two mild surprises: one is that the elder son of the right sort of rich man had something like a claim to be on the bench;

the other is that this elder son was lucky not to have had this presumption over-ridden by his illegitimacy. At least the first of these views of the matter would have obtained at any time before the late nineteenth century.

The last hundred years of Quarter Sessions saw three changes of prime significance which, taken together, transformed its role and operation. The first and most important came not long after Trollope's time, in the late nineteenth century. It was brought about by the construction and reconstruction of local government effected by statutes of 1888 and later. The effect of this legislation was to transfer the administrative functions of Quarter Sessions to the newly established county councils, and for the control of the police outside London to be managed by the two in conjunction. (The control of the Metropolitan Police had been assigned, on its establishment sixty years earlier, to Commissioners responsible to the Home Secretary). From now on, Quarter Sessions was a court of law and little else.

A Liberal government with a large majority took office in 1906. The property qualification for the magistracy was abolished soon afterwards. A Royal Commission reported in 1910 and, in line with its report, advisory committees were established for every commission area to make recommendations on appointments. This has remained the procedure. A further change, and an important one, was made by an Act of 1938 which made it possible for a court of Quarter Sessions to obtain enhanced powers if it chose to ask the Lord Chancellor to assign to it a legally qualified chairman. Something like this had for many years obtained in Middlesex, though nowhere else, as in Middlesex the volume and kind of work were such as to require the nearly permanent sitting of the court and legally qualified chairmanship. Before 1938 the chair in court was taken by a magistrate, whether on account of his chancing to have legal qualifications, or on grounds of seniority or of his general acceptability. The option now presented was widely taken up. After this, the distinction between Assizes and Quarter Sessions must have come to seem anachronistic and explicable only on historical grounds. Both were now courts presided over by professional lawyers. Their abolition, by way of merger, in 1971 is therefore unsurprising. If it had not been for the concurrent, if slow-paced, development of Petty Sessions, this would have been the end of the lay magistracy.

Petty Sessions

There is no single date in history, corresponding to 1361, for the origin of Petty Sessions. The least misleading thing to say is that in the early nineteenth century a distinct form of magistrates' court came to be regulated by a succession of Parliamentary statutes. This came at a late point in a long development. It had long been the practice for the county magistrates to meet in smaller groups between meetings of Quarter Sessions to deal with matters relating to their own parts of that county. Over the same period, Parliament had assigned a large miscellany of responsibilities and powers to justices of the peace, for exercise out of Quarter Sessions, whether individually or in pairs. For a long time, there was no prescription how these new statutory functions should be exercised, and the magistrates seem to have been left to settle this for themselves. In due course, it came to be recognised that a pared-down magistrates' court, with limited powers, had come into being. By way of distinction from Quarter Sessions, it came to be styled Petty Sessions. Later (in 1889) Petty Sessions was defined by statute as, 'A court of summary jurisdiction consisting of two or more Justices sitting in a petty sessional courthouse.' 'Summary' denotes the absence of a jury: it was always for the justices alone to determine fact and law. Over the course of the nineteenth century such courts came to acquire their own clerks and premises and the other familiar marks of a 'bench'. Maitland noted that in 1881 the number of petty sessional divisions was 715 (*Justice and Police*, 1885). Throughout, Quarter Sessions continued as before, its justices coming to sit both at that level and at the level below. In this way, a decided innovation came about gradually and (it seems) with little notice. Maitland remarked that it was 'yearly becoming of greater importance'.

In the earlier stages of this process, we can imagine the single justice doing justice or discharging other functions in a room in a manor house set aside for the purpose. He would have done so with little formality and so at the risk of some arbitrariness. In time, he would have had written guidance in the shape of manuals published for the purpose: by the time of the eighteenth century there were several of these. This was all the guidance on the law the justice would have had unless he had supplemented it with the advice of a clerk with some legal knowledge, for which he would have had to pay himself. He may, of course, as I have suggested, have had some legal education in his youth. Justices and their clerks were often empowered to take fees for the discharge of their statutory functions. Here was at least an opening to corruption. I touch below on the dubious reputation of the Middlesex justices in the eighteenth century and their consequent replacement in London by stipendiary magistrates.

The modern reader is likely to be struck more by the harshness of much of what was done than by plain injustice or corruption. The diary of the Reverend James Woodforde, a country clergyman in Norfolk in the late eighteenth century, records his conducting of the marriage of a most unwilling young man to a young woman whom the man was said to have made pregnant. The procedure would have been that laid down by the Bastardy

140

Act of 1733. A local justice would have figured in it. It ensured that the local ratepayers would be spared the cost of maintaining the child, as the alleged father, now married to the mother, would have been made responsible. The diarist records his sense that this was 'a cruel thing' and records that he found his own part in it 'very disagreeable'. He seems however to have taken it for granted that he had to play that part. We are left to wonder how far the magistrate, of whom nothing is said, shared the vicar's sentiments.

Fictional treatments of magistrates discharging this sort of role are often derisive and often ring true. The most memorable is that of Justice Shallow, his colleague and his clerk in Shakespeare's play, *King Henry IV Part Two*. This is especially telling from coming in a play which also contains a glowingly complimentary portrait of a judge. The two justices are probably acting under a commission of muster and not under the commission of the peace, but the former would in all probability have been composed largely of justices . Who else would have been available and suitable? In the play, we can make out the basic elements of a court of petty sessions, as it was to come to be, in the form of two justices and their clerk. We also get a clear view, and not a pleasant one, of how Justice Shallow would have discharged his magisterial functions from the way he goes about his immediate task of raising troops. The colleague is merely senile. Centuries later, we find in *Pickwick Papers* a rendering of the pomposity and incompetence of a justice of the peace of Dickens' day. Mr Nupkins has to be put right by his clerk every time he makes a mistake, which is all the time.

Dickens fastens here on a supposed weakness in the lay magistracy which at least until recently was often brought up, that magistrates were far too dependent on their clerks, to the extent of allowing them to run their courts. What comes out is a difficulty – and a very obvious one – in the operation of the lay magistracy which has been evident from the beginning: how are those with no legal qualifications, yet with a judicial role, to be advised on the law? There was, at one and the same time, a risk of the justices having none of the advice they needed, and the opposite risk that they might be the passive recipients of direction dressed up as advice. Earlier chapters have shown that this remains a sensitive point.

With the development of Petty Sessions, the mode of trial of criminal offences became two-fold: summary and indictable. Petty Sessions dealt with the numerous offences created by Parliamentary statute which provided that they should be tried summarily – that is, that guilt should be determined and sentence passed, by a bench of justices or by a stipendiary magistrate. Indictable offences – the more serious – had to be tried at Quarter Sessions or Assizes and the verdict delivered by a jury. It is these that are now tried at the Crown Court. In time, there came to be a third and intermediate category, that of 'either-way' offences. An Act of Parliament sometimes made it possible for a specified indictable offence to be tried at Petty Sessions if two conditions were satisfied: after hearing what a particular charge amounted to, the magistrates had to find it suitable to be dealt with in this way, and the defendant had to agree to summary trial. Maitland recorded the marking out of this new category and saw its significance for the future. Since then, the category has been much enlarged, notably by the Criminal Justice Act of 1925. Many of the offences which I have discussed in earlier chapters will have been 'either way'.

In sum, the magistrates' court of today is the court of Petty Sessions as it developed over the last two and a half centuries and with its roots in earlier centuries. It grew up under cover of Quarter Sessions and the extension of its jurisdiction to cover 'either-way' offences has given it much of the weight and importance of Quarter Sessions.

The Stipendiary Magistracy

Something must be said about the origins of the stipendiary magistracy if one of the oddest features of our system of summary justice – odd at least to the outside observer – is to be understood. The introduction of stipendiary magistrates is best explained as an attempt to address some endemic social inadequacies. London had an adequate, or at least fully functional, government in the City – that is, in the original London. Outside the City, local government and the system of law enforcement were over-burdened and out of date. The problem was aggravated by the inadequacy and corruption widely attributed to the Middlesex county justices . Middlesex was one of the smallest counties in England, while London was by far the largest urban area; London so overwhelmed Middlesex that what worked passably well elsewhere had become impossible here. In other words, there was nothing corresponding to the by-and-large sound and solid county gentry who filled the commission of the peace elsewhere. Appointments to the bench were poor, it seemed irremediably so.

The remedy adopted was to appoint well-qualified justices who would give all their time to the work, which would have been taken to be law-enforcement rather than essentially judicial. As has been brought out above, the distinction of the two was then nothing like as plain as it has come to be. Those appointed would receive a stipend – that is, a salary – for the work and would not take fees. The ability to require fees was an obvious opening for corruption. One of the first and the most famous of stipendiary magistrates was the novelist, Henry Fielding, the author of *Tom Jones* and other things. Fielding was a barrister before he was a novelist, and had been a justice of the peace both for the county of Middlesex and on the 'borough' bench of Westminster. Quite late in his not very long life, Fielding came to work as a magistrate full time and for a salary. He refers in passing to this work, and in an enlightening way, in his last book, *The Journal of a Voyage to Lisbon*, published after his death. We can see from these passing remarks, as Fielding in all probability could not, that he is marking the emergence of a different kind of judicial agent.

In the same book, Fielding refers to his friend, Saunders Welch, who succeeded him and his younger half-brother, Sir John Fielding, in this new role. Welch must have been a remarkable man: 'Mr Welch, whom I never think or speak of but with love and esteem,' wrote Henry Fielding. He seems to have been born in poverty. Apprenticed as a boy to a trunk-maker, he was for many years a grocer. He became a justice for Westminster and, more remarkably, also for the county of Middlesex. Eighteenth century government cannot have been as class-bound as is sometimes suggested. What Welch's career makes plain is that the stipendiary magistrate was in origin a justice of the peace picked out from the mass to deal with special problems, rather than a magistrate with special qualifications who might in time supersede those without them.

The experiment of strengthening the magistracy through the appointment of a very few salaried and expert justices might easily have lapsed. It must have persisted because it continued to be found necessary. It was extended and formalised fifty years later, with the establishment by statute of a fixed number of stipendiary magistrates for the metropolitan area. Conditions in London being what they were, experience must have shown the necessity of this bolstering of forces. It was only some time after this that special – that is, legal – qualifications came to be judged essential. Not until 1839 was it prescribed that the stipendiary magistrate should be a barrister. Here was the real breach with the past.

The metropolitan stipendiary bench operated within a defined area in central London outside the City. It co-existed across this area with the lay magistracy, and the relationship between the two was – unsurprisingly – somewhat uncertain. The intention of successive Home Secretaries, certainly that of Peel in the 1820s, may well have been that it should replace rather than supplement the lay bench. To have provided for outright replacement by statute would however have been a step too far for the conservative temper of the times. The outcome was well summarised by Sir Alexander Maxwell, a former permanent head of the Home Office, in evidence given to the Royal Commission which reported in 1948:

> 'Peel's object was to oust the lay justices and to prevent them from acting…and in order to do that he had first of all to instruct the police that they were not to take cases before lay Justices , and also to indicate in an Act of Parliament that the lay justices should not be entitled to any fees for any work they chose to do.'

The outcome fell short of what Peel, on this account, wished for, in that the lay bench retained its role in respects other than the summary disposition of criminal matters. It was never formally excluded even from these. It simply became the practice of the police, in line with Peel's supposed intention, to present offenders to stipendiary magistrates. It must have been this which led to them becoming known as 'police magistrates' and their courts as 'police courts'. As a label, this now seems decidedly unfortunate, suggesting that stipendiary magistrates and the police were somehow on the same side, suggesting even that at a 'police court' someone charged could expect to be tried by the police.

Metropolitan stipendiary magistrates were not badly paid. After 1839, the chief metropolitan magistrate received an annual 'stipend' or salary of £1,400 and the remainder, to a maximum of twenty seven, one of £1,200. This was at a time when £800 a year was a decidedly respectable middle class income. It was therefore misleading to suggest that only a plain failure at the Bar would have taken the job though, no doubt, the notably successful or ambitious would not have taken it, nor anyone looking for intellectual stimulus. Stipendiary magistrates were appointed by the Home Secretary, with the consequence that, at least in the eighteenth and nineteenth centuries, appointment was by way of informal patronage and that political allegiance counted for much. This was the case with all public appointments, including those to the judiciary, and was by and large taken for granted. There were also a few stipendiary magistrates who sat outside London. Their appointment was at the request of a local authority and was brought about by the same process. The local authorities were responsible for their payment, which is no doubt why there were no more and also why their appointment was often intermittent.

The lay magistracy remained the norm: it was the almost invariable form of tribunal for the discharge of summary justice. The co-existence of a salaried and professionally qualified magistracy was however enough to point up its singularity. The oddity of the dealing out of justice by 'three successful tradesmen' would have seemed all the more striking if the tradesmen were in some important respects not up to the job.

Adversarial and Inquisitorial

Over the latter part of the period which I have marked out – after about 1700 – there were developments in the conduct of the criminal trial which in time served to give the judges' role a distinctive character, in one perspective a surprising one. The role of magistrates came to be determined in the same way. These developments were not inevitable, and continental legal systems know little of them. In sum, they brought about a recasting of the criminal process into a so-called 'adversarial' form.

These developments have been set out in an illuminating way by an American scholar, Professor John H Langbein (*The Origins of Adversary Criminal Trial*, 2003). This exhaustive study, drawing largely on the records of the Old Bailey, covers the period from the 1690s to the point in the early nineteenth century at which a Continental observer, quoted by Langbein, could remark on the way English judges had to a great extent given up the conduct of their own proceedings. We could put this development another way by saying that they had become referees rather than interrogators. The change came about only slowly. Langbein describes the shift from permitting the defendant no legal representation, through the stages at which this was conceded to him to an increasing degree, to the point at which the criminal trial had come to resemble a duel between professionals, victory – in the form of a verdict – being awarded by a jury subject to the judge's directions on the law. It was part of this development that the defendant was no longer exposed to being required to answer in his own person to the charges that had been put to him. Earlier, this requirement had been at the centre of the process. The change was therefore almost a reversal. Once established in the higher courts, the new process came inevitably to be that of the 'lower' – that is, of magistrates' – courts also. It obtained whether or not the defendant was legally represented: when he was not, he had to be, as it were, his own representative; he continued, and continues, to be spared direct questioning unless he chose to go into the witness box.

The merits of this fundamental change in process are open to argument (Langbein is decidedly critical). That argument cannot be pursued here, but the change has to be mentioned here as it bore and still bears largely on the role of lay magistrates, making that role one they should be well able to discharge. It fits well with English common law's assignment of the burden of proof to the prosecutor and with its setting of the standard of proof at such a high point, 'beyond reasonable doubt' or 'so as to be sure'. The court's responsibility is to judge whether a charge has been made out, not to work out to its own satisfaction what happened on a particular occasion. To quote from the lay magistrate's handbook, *Anthony and Berryman*, successor to a long line of such layman's guides:

> 'When an accused person enters a not guilty plea, he is not necessarily proclaiming his innocence. This arises from two factors: first, it is not the function of the court whether he is guilty or not, the court's function is to decide *whether the prosecutor has proved that he is guilty*. Second, there may be legal or procedural reasons why an accused should enter a not guilty plea...' (*Anthony and Berryman's* emphasis)

In other words, the court's business is proof rather than – directly – truth.

There are many people who would argue that this is not as it should be, wishing to substitute an inquisitorial system which would be designed to establish the truth. (For a recent statement of this point of view, see Chapter Seven above). Whether or not they are justified in this preference, the words I have quoted are hardly open to challenge as a summary of the law as it stands. I quote them only to enforce the point that what magistrates conducting a trial have to do is, if not exactly simple, at least clear-cut. The demands placed on them should be well within their competence. 'Has the charge been made out?' is a question to which there should always be an answer. If the bench has been left bemused, the charge has not been made out and acquittal should follow.

Magistrates generally prefer defendants to be legally represented at their trial, as the justice taking the chair and the clerk will then be spared a task which otherwise falls to them, the clerk normally taking the larger part. This is to assist the unrepresented defendant in putting his case and (much the same thing) in his rebuttal of the prosecution case, without seeming to suggest a line of defence of their own devising or in any way to prompt him. This is taxing and not easily managed. In its difficulty, we can see that it is in some ways similar to that direct interrogation of the defendant – that calling on him to explain his actions – which is no longer permitted, unless of course he or she chooses to enter the witness box and give sworn evidence. The resemblance is enough to show how much more onerous the obligation to interrogate the defendant directly would be. If criminal process had developed differently, without the sharp move to the adversarial, it is hard to suppose that the lay magistracy would not have been superseded long ago.

9.

1948 and After

How it Was in 1948

The Labour government elected in 1945 followed the precedent of the Liberal government of 1906 in establishing a Royal Commission to consider the lay magistracy. This second Royal Commission was charged specifically with considering the appointment and removal of magistrates and with recommending a procedure by which 'only the most suitable persons are appointed'; it was also also 'to consider and report generally'. This last part of its charge permitted a general view of the performance of the lay magistracy, and to a modest degree the Commission's report offered this. Its report was however focussed on the procedure for appointment. Since 1910, successive Lord Chancellors had made appointments only after receiving the recommendation of advisory committees. It seems to have been widely held that there had been many poor appointments to the bench and that this was attributable to the party political bias of these committtees.

The evidence provided to the second Royal Commission provides a useful conspectus of views on the subject of the magistracy and of summary justice more generally, at least of those views held by the respectable. I have drawn on this in what follows and will draw also on a polemical book entitled *English Justice*, published anonymously in 1932 and reissued in paperback more than once. The author appears on the title page as 'Solicitor', and it is obvious why someone still practising in magistrates' courts would have wished for anonymity. Taken together, the two sources provide a vivid impression of how things were in the interwar period and up to the 1940s. This shows how greatly they were to be changed for the better over the next forty years and how adaptable the lay magistracy could be when it needed to be. Here is something which permits a hopeful view of the future.

"Solicitor' says bluntly that it was probable that the quality of lay magistrates can seldom have been worse. (He refers to how things were around 1930). He is highly critical of the way in which business was quite often done, and says so, though he grants that there were many conscientious magistrates and clerks along with the bad ones. He is careful to avoid idealising the past, conceding that those on the bench before the changes of 1910 were often narrow-minded and class-biased. He claims however that 'they had at least a considerable experience in dealing with men and weighing evidence'. He claims also that appointment by the advisory committees had produced benches with less sense of responsibility and respect for the law than their predecessors had possessed, and which were over-influenced by the police and by their clerks. He attributes this to appointment on the basis of party loyalty – he must have had in mind Labour Party loyalty. Comparing past and present, 'Solicitor' notes:

> 'The clerk, too, seldom dominated the court as he usually does at the present time. He was formerly as a rule the social inferior, as he is now usually the superior, of his justices.'

Those who gave evidence to the second Royal Commission are mostly in broad agreement with 'Solicitor', though without the cover of anonymity they express themselves more delicately. This makes what 'Solicitor' says too persuasive to be dismissed as merely snobbish. Lord Maugham, a former Lord Chancellor, wanted more working men on the bench but not, it seems, those appointed on the basis of party political loyalty; he said that the advisory committee system should be modified to ensure this. Sir Theobald Matthew, the Director of Public Prosecutions, declared that the advisory committees should be:

> 'as representative of all classes of the community as possible but the people they recommend should not be selected ostensibly for any political, religious or representative reason.'

Other witnesses declared that the system, as it had operated, had produced benches which were broadly balanced in political allegiance, and that the point which had seemed most urgent in 1910 had been met. They judged however that the advisory committees' approach had had the effect of leaving off the bench many of those whose contribution would have strengthened it, who had been left out of consideration because they carried no party political label.

'Solicitor's' point of observation seems to have been that of the practitioner, well placed, as he waits for his case to be called on, to observe how other defendants are mistreated both by the bench and the clerk. He claims that all too often defendants, and especially unrepresented defendants, are treated high-handedly and that the magistrates' task is discharged superficially and with prejudice. On his account, many magistrates lack both a proper sense of duty and an adequate grasp of natural justice:

> 'Magistrates are apt to think that their main duty is to convict and punish guilty persons, and that the rules of evidence and procedure which they have sworn to observe are mere red tape, hindering them in their work. Not only do most of them make no attempt to rid their minds of what they know about a case

before proceeding to hear it, but they pride themselves on their inside information, and pass it on to their colleagues...'

This takes us to the heart of what 'Solicitor' found to be wrong, the propensity of many lay magistrates, not chosen for their judicial temperament, to presume the guilt of those who appeared before them. He says bluntly that there were many unsafe and plainly wrong convictions. There would no doubt have been fewer if more defendants had had legal representation, though 'Solicitor' does not make too much of that. Even represented defendants often had a bad time. The provision of legal aid was severely limited in the interwar period and it was available only at the discretion of the court. He asserts:

'The Poor Prisoners Defence Act is a farce so far as the police courts are concerned, but a criminal, even if hard up, can generally contrive to be defended. The innocent do not know the ropes.'

He adds in a footnote:

'In 1938 1,044 Courts of Summary Jurisdiction between them granted 329 Legal Aid Certificates. Magistrates do not like defended cases.'

This last comment may be unfair. Legal aid was an innovation, designed only for the exceptional case. Magistrates can hardly be blamed for sharing the presumption of the time in favour of strict economy in the public sphere. The governments in power in the interwar period would never have accepted the large expansion of provision which was to come about. Nonetheless, an over-hasty and corner-cutting procedure in contested cases must often have led to miscarriages of justice. A larger supply of combative lawyers would have helped.

The Royal Commission's main recommendation was therefore unsurprising, if arguably more cautious than it needed to be. It was to continue the system of appointment on the recommendation of advisory committees. These committees should be a cross-section of the population of commission-areas and composed of those with good local knowledge. Their membership should not be made public, but the identity of their secretaries should be disclosed, so that anyone could suggest names for consideration. The suggestion often made, that those under consideration should be interviewed, did not find favour. The committees need not disregard party political allegiance altogether, but the weight given to this factor should be restricted. They should be charged with recommending those best qualified for appointment, departing from this only with a view to avoiding the preponderance of one party.

The Royal Commission's other main recommendations represented a pragmatic response to the criticisms most often and most forcefully put to it. Magistrates should receive some instruction in their duties. There should be a retiring-age of 75. The advisory committees should review benches annually with a view to cutting out magistrates who were ineffective, notably in failing to attend with the necessary frequency. Each bench was to elect a chairman by secret ballot; the chairman would serve as the point of communication with central and local government. Some expenses would be payable; they would extend to travelling-costs and lodging allowances, but not to subsistence or compensation for loss of earnings. These recommendations can now be seen to contain in germ the much more thoroughgoing changes of the next sixty years.

Fom the perspective of the twenty-first century, it may seem surprising that the Royal Commission of 1948 made such moderate recommendations for change. Its terms of reference did not require it to consider more far-reaching options, but they would have permitted this, and one member took advantage of the opportunity. What is plain is that there was no appetite for basic change. The anonymous solicitor, who might have been expected to be more radical, was against change on the essential point of perpetuating the lay magistracy. It was very widely held in 1948 that there was no readily achievable alternative. At the same time, we find arguments of principle made for the *status quo*, both from those who gave evidence and from 'Solicitor'. For the present, he can have the last word:

> 'It is of the first importance to retain the lay element in the administration of the law. That representatives of the ordinary citizen should not only know what is being done, but take part in doing it, is vitally necessary. Without this… the administration of justice will fall into the hands of a priest-craft, or of experts, if you prefer the term.'

Since 1948

The lay magistracy has changed greatly over the sixty years which have followed the Royal Commission's report, both in its make-up and organisation and in the way it discharges its role. In historical perspective, the abolition of Quarter Sessions was the greatest change, certainly the sharpest break with the past. It has turned out to be even more of a break than might have been foreseen in 1971. For a time, justices of the peace retained something of a role in the operation of the new Crown Court which replaced Quarter Sessions and Assizes. All that now remains to them is to sit with judges or recorders to hear appeals from magistrates' courts, against verdict or sentence or both. This is plainly desirable. The presence of lay magistrates on the bench ensures that such appeals are heard by a tribunal containing persons familiar with minor matters, as judges and recorders are unlikely to be.

As for the day-to-day running of magistrates' courts, this is now much more tightly organised. The allocation of sittings by way of rota is now the norm. The numerous small commission-areas of seventy years ago were reduced in number, first by way of amalgamation, and finally and only recently, with the passage of the Courts Act of 2007, by way of abolishing commissions. This radical change, after over six centuries, passed without fuss and with little notice. The essential change had already come about. Its formalisation can now be seen to follow naturally from the abolition of Quarter Sessions. Appointment is now directly to the magistracy or *as* a magistrate or Justice of the Peace – which means the same thing – and not to any commission. At the same time, those newly appointed continue to be allocated to what is now called a 'local justice area'. This is, in effect, the territory of the bench to which magistrates will see themselves as belonging. The numerical strength of these local benches varies considerably. It may be less than a hundred, though probably more than fifty, and may as much as several hundred.

Clerks are now employed to work full-time, and are public servants, employed by Her Majesty's Courts and Tribunals Service (HMCTS), an emanation of the Ministry of Justice. Before that, though paid from public funds, they were in the employment of local committees, drawn largely from the magistracy. When this change was in contemplation, there was some concern among magistrates that the independence of those who gave them advice on the law might be compromised by those advisors becoming, effectively, civil servants. Suppose a minister were to attempt to manipulate lay magistrates, by way of directing their clerks on some sensitive point of law? Here is an important point which might well have struck the observant foreigner whom I imagined as a critic earlier in this chapter. There were reassurances from ministers on the point, and I know of nothing to suggest that this danger has become real. The subject of legal aid is highly topical. It requires separate treatment, which could not be brief. The scope of debate is much wider than that of this book, as legal aid is available in civil as well as criminal proceedings and at all levels. I mention it here only because it is too important to be simply ignored.

Very many of those in whose trials I participated would have received legal aid. I could not be unaware of the cost to public funds, though my direct concern was very slight. Whatever the resources available, if there is to be any legal aid there will always be two criteria for its award: the need for representation in the interests of justice and the need for assistance on grounds of absolute or relative poverty. Arrangements varied, but for most of my time on the bench, it was the practice for the decision on the interests of justice criterion – often not a easy one – to be taken by a designated subordinate of the Justices' Clerk, with the applicant having the right of appeal to the court – that is, to a district judge or a bench. Such appeals were rare. The means criterion was more easily applied. There was a scale: those whose financial resources fell below a certain point could be granted legal aid and required to contribute nothing; those whose resources were above some other and higher point would receive nothing. A sliding scale would be applied to the large category in between.

As we have seen, legal aid was available in magistrates' courts in the inter-war period, but only to a very limited extent. It cannot have cost much. Since 1949, and especially more recently, the cost to the public purse has become considerable. In a consultation document published in 2010, the incoming Justice

Secretary declared: 'The current scheme... has expanded, so much so that it is now one of the most expensive in the world, available for a very wide range of issues, including some which should no require any legal expertise to resolve...' Subsequent legislation has made the means-testing much more rigorous and competition has been introduced into the pricing of legal services.

The reaction from both branches of the legal profession has been strong and hostile; there have been demonstrations and a form of strike action. To quote from a letter to *The Independent* in June 2015:

> 'I am a junior barrister and my practice consists exclusively of privately funded civil work. I earn £27,000 pa. No pension, no sick pay, no paid holidays. My colleagues practising in criminal and family law are often paid considerably less. They are leaving the profession in droves.

> It is no longer possible for a working-class person without family money to consider a career in publicly funded law. They are frequently expected to spend a day in court for less than the cost of the train fare to get there – literally paying to work. There has been no increase in legal aid rates of pay since 1995, and rates have been cut several times since then...'

My feelings on this are ambivalent. What is claimed in this letter is perfectly credible and the state of affairs it describes cannot be in the public interest. At the same time, I recall many occasions where I had a strong sense of extravagance. A defence might be presented, sometimes by a barrister with a firm of solicitors behind him, which seemed so thin that it hardly counted as a defence. When the defendant's means were laid bare, on his or her inevitable conviction, it became clear that he had no money and could not have been required to contribute anything to the cost of his defence. A proper application of the interests of justice criterion should have excluded such cases, but not a few got past it. My tentative conclusion is that some reform of the legal aid system is inevitable and proper.

Appointments to the lay magistracy continue to be made by the Lord Chancellor on the recommendation of advisory committees though now with the concurrence of the Lord Chief Justice. Recommendation is not quite tantamount to appointment. In a volume of memoirs (*The Door Wherein I Went,*1975), Lord Hailsham, both a former and a future Lord Chancellor, recorded that he occasionally rejected a name, though he never added one. In effect, however, the bench of magistrates is appointed by the advisory committees. The committees are composed in large part of experienced magistrates, along with judges and other persons in public life, chosen by the Lord Chancellor with a view to diversity of experience. I have already given some account of the appointment procedure, in describing my own experience.

Once an appointment has been made and the new recruit has been sworn in, he or she begins a course of 'training', a mixture of attendance at court as an observer with a group of others, of reading, of being lectured at, of discussing hypothetical cases in large or small groups, and of visits to prisons. The 'trainers' will usually be Justices' Clerks or their staff or district judges. All this is so much part of modern life that further description seems unnecessary. 'Training' is not confined to new recruits, but is part of the routine of the active magistrate. When the criminal law is changed, as it is with fair frequency, or when there are broader changes such as the passage of the Human Rights Act of 1998, courses will be laid on and magistrates exhorted, and sometimes required, to attend them. Sometimes there are talks by probation officers – that is, staff of the National Offender Management Service – by members of the police, and by criminologists. There are also courses on parts of their duties which magistrates may have found problematic. Much of this is conducted under the aegis of a committee made up of magistrates and specially charged with training and development. There is one of these for each local justice area.

The impulse for this seems to have come from the Royal Commission's report, though its scope has become much wider than the Royal Commission envisaged. Addressing the question of 'suitability' for service on the bench, it reported:

'What is often called unsuitability is in fact lack of knowledge. Judicial conduct is not assured by intellectual ability or even by the possession of a suitable temperament; it is a specialised discipline or technique that has to be learned.'

The uncompromising tone of this, as much as the content, might have surprised many of even the more conscientious magistrates of the past. It is now hard to imagine it being seriously questioned.

Along with 'training' goes appraisal. Magistrates are now appraised by other magistrates in respect of their performance – that is, the discharge of their duties in court. The appraisers themselves will have been instructed how to go about this. A record of each appraisal goes to the training and development committee which each bench now has, which may propose remedial action. This would be the first stage of a process which may lead to a recommendation that a magistrate should cease to be one on the ground that his performance was unacceptably poor and apparently beyond improvement. This procedure was brought in around 1990 for those who took the chair in court and is now required of everyone. Experienced magistrates will be appraised every three years or so; for those recently appointed it is more frequent and those wishing to take the chair will only do so on a regular basis if they have been appraised and found by the committee to be up to the task.

The Human Rights Act was enacted in 1998. Much could be said about this measure, but all that is relevant here is that it places on public bodies the obligation to give effect to the European Convention on Human Rights. A magistrates' court counts as a public body, and the consequences of this obligation may be very far-reaching. A whole range of possibilities has been opened up. At some unexpected point in their handling of a matter, a bench of three lay magistrates or a district judge may have their attention drawn to the Act, and a submission made to them that they should take some step which, unprompted, they would never have thought of. An instance of that would be finding that the Act of Parliament which defined the offence with which they were concerned was, in part, incompatible with the Convention. Such occasions have however been most infrequent. Most magistrates will do little more than brush up against human rights in the normal course of duty.

The passage of the Human Rights Act of has however been the prompt for one change in the handling of cases which is of prime importance. Magistrates must now give a statement of their reasons for decisions, notably for reaching a verdict – Guilty or Not Guilty – in a disputed case. Previously, all a defendant might receive was the bare utterance of one or other of these formulae. He or she and any one else concerned was left to guess at the court's reasons. This rule of silence, as it must have seemed, was not applied consistently. Outrage at a particular set of facts might be the spur to an expression of the court's view of the matter, but this might be no more than the chairman's own view, unshared by those sitting with him, and it might be confused and verbose. It is now the practice for the bench to agree on a summary of its reasons for a decision, to give these reasons a preliminary written form and to invite the views of the clerk on the adequacy of the summary, though not on the substance of the decision. It may then be amended, for the chairman to read it out in court and for the clerk to preserve it. That this procedure is preferable hardly needs arguing. Its greatest merit is its enforcement of a discipline of thought. The drafting of a statement of reasons should ensure that the decision emerges as the outcome of an intellectual process.

By slow stages and in almost every way, the lay magistracy has been transformed over the past sixty years. An appreciable change to the most conspicuous part of the system of criminal justice has come about with little public notice. It has not been the subject of party political contention and has proceeded steadily through the terms of government of both large parties. It may be summed up as being one of making the lay magistracy 'professional', but oddly professional, in ways I will try to bring out in what follows. All this makes the role and status of a justice of the peace something other than what it was a hundred years ago. Though this considerable change is certainly largely for the better, I believe it has come at something of a price. I will try to explain why I think this in what follows.

10.

How it Stands with
The Lay Magistracy

On my appointment to the bench in 1989, I came quite quickly to see that the morale of quite a few of my new colleagues was less buoyant than it should have been. This surprised me, as I was aware how greatly the magistracy, and especially the lay magistracy, had changed over the previous half century and how well it had accommodated change. Here were good grounds for a modest self-assurance. Such assurance seemed lacking. Instead, I registered a self-defensiveness, even a sense of grievance. This came out in casual talk in the retiring room or in the routine formal meetings of magistrates, and could often be found in the proceedings and publications of The Magistrates' Association.

The interest and importance of at least a fair proportion of the work which falls to lay magistrates and to their professional colleagues should have been evident from the earlier chapters of this book. The proportion seems likely to grow. The enlargement of the 'either way' category and the outright withdrawal of the right to trial by jury for some offences have had this effect, and the trend seems likely to continue. The pressure from above is for magistrates to take on more work from the Crown Court along with extended sentencing powers. Why then was there this sense of vulnerability and of being open to supersession? The explanation is not straightforward.

Legal advisors

The role of magistrates' clerks has been transformed over a long period. We have seen that it had its origin in the employment of clerks by individual magistrates. This led to their employment on a regular basis, though often still part-time, by local benches; it has ended with the effective transference of the clerks' function to the public service. The transformation has been one from dependency to equality: the lay magistrate of today does his work within the context supplied by a boarded-out part of the government machine.

Along with this development, and in all likelihood as a consequence of it, there has come to be a slow but noticeable enlargement of the clerks' role. The listing-function is a notable instance of this. The importance of listing – that is, the working out of which cases go where – will be obvious; it involves – among much else – the division of work between justices and district judges. Listing is now left to the clerks. This means that the assignment of each item of business is determined, at least initially, by the senior clerk for each courthouse or, in practice, by his or her subordinate staff. It is still feasible for a district judge or a lay bench with a matter before them for which a second or later listing will be necessary to require that it should be re-assigned on that later occasion to him, her or them. This quite often happens, and it is highly desirable that it should: there are obvious advantages in a case being dealt with throughout by the same person or people. It is most commonly done when the sentencing of an offender has to be deferred, usually for a report to be prepared. Here we get a glimpse of what must have been the original way of organising a court's business, with the justices themselves determining the distribution and processing of work. In time, this came to be left largely to the court-staff, by way of delegation from the justices . It will now be taken for granted on all sides that it is part of the court-staff's job.

A smaller and more recent instance of the enlargement of the legal advisors' role is their empowerment to grant adjournments in cases where neither side opposes this. This is not a supersession of the magistrates' role in granting adjournments, but the establishment of another beside it. It is not uncommon for a bench in its retiring room, engaged on something else, to be informed by its clerk that they can disregard a case on its list which has yet to be called on, the clerk having just adjourned it. This small modification of procedure must often result in the saving of the time of busy people – solicitors and counsel having to hang around – but the magistrates of the past might have found it disturbing, even if their successors do not. It is an instance of a larger trend for legal advisors to be permitted to exercise the powers of a lay magistrate sitting solo. As a small change in procedure, it may be unexceptionable; the question is whether the trend should be welcomed.

Another instance is the now common formalisation of the legal advisor's role on occasions when a search warrant or a warrant under the Mental Health Act is applied for out-of-hours. In Chapter Six, I gave some account of this procedure. The bench on which I served did not then provide for applications by the police to be submitted through a clerk and it was left to the justice who received an application to seek a clerk's advice if it seemed to be needed. For my own part, I made a point of checking with a clerk that it was within my powers to grant the application. Once this was confirmed, it was up to me to consider a set of facts or to appraise the application's urgency. In doing this, even when it was difficult, as it commonly was not, the task seemed to be mine alone.

This part of a justice's work is exceptional in that it falls to be discharged, not only without a legal advisor at hand, but alone and without the support of other justices . It is understandable that lay magistrates, especially to start with, will look for a steer. General advice in written form is of course available from more than one source. It is impossible to look at this advice – which is often more instruction than advice – without coming to see that the way I (and others) handled applications was regarded as hazardous by senior clerks and others in the Court Service. The unspoken assumption was that the sole and unsupported lay magistrate cannot be trusted not to go wrong. To quote from the most commonly employed *vade mecum*, Anthony and Berryman's *Magistrates' Court Guide* (2008 edition): 'If that [deferring the application until it can be made in court] is not possible, the Justices' Clerk or a legal advisor should be telephoned for advice. The following notes are intended to give a broad description of the procedure. *They should not be taken to encourage the hearing of an application in the absence of a legal advisor.*' (emphasis in original)

The procedure of my own previous bench has now been modified to ensure that applications are put through a clerk. As I noted in Chapter Six, it is decidedly unusual for an application to be refused – much too unusual, I have suggested. The new procedure seems to make the magistrate all the more someone who signs as a matter of course, as it may easily lead him to suppose that if the application was a dubious one the clerk would have blocked its submission. Everything seems set for the further amendment of procedure which would permit the clerk to sign the warrant. Should this come about, it would amount to another small shift within the relationship.

Few lay magistrates, in my experience, see any threat to what matters in their position in these developments, and I am myself not sure that they are detrimental. This reaction – or lack of reaction – is probably attributable to lay magistrates' broad satisfaction with things as they are. The day-to-day relationship of lay magistrates and legal advisors is, in my experience, nearly always at least passably effective. Quite often I came to the end of a day in court with a bracing sense of how strong the relationship often was and how much this contributed to the court's work being done well. This strength came largely from the acquaintance which came about from the two sides' working together regularly and developing respect for the other's contribution.

This happy state is not of course always realised. In Chapter Five, I gave some account of the rare occasions within my own experience on which the proper relationship between lay magistrate and clerk broke down temporarily. It hardly needs saying that there will be more frequent occasions where this is merely strained. The strain is usually between the court-clerk and the justice taking the chair, and is probably inescapable; both parties will be moved, in all likelihood, by a true concern for doing justice, unhappily mixed up with *amour propre*. This is a toxic combination, which makes it difficult for either party to give way.

District Judges

When lay magistrates complain about a weakening of their position, whether by way of an invasion of their proper sphere or otherwise, the single fact on which they are mostly likely to fasten is a fairly recent sharp increase in the number of district judges, as stipendiary magistrates are now known. This complaint is regularly heard in the publications and other proceedings of The Magistrates' Association. In 1999, half way through my service, I recorded:

'... Magistrates' Association meeting addressed by the Chief Metropolitan Magistrate (Parkinson): The Future of the Magistracy in Inner London. A good address, bringing out the way in which our future is likely to be uncomfortable in the interests of economy. Questions afterwards, in which the widespread fear among justices of being squeezed out or subordinated by stipendiaries, in part on the same financial grounds, becomes painfully clear. Parkinson is good on this, not trying to ingratiate himself with his audience.'

There has been some lobbying of successive Lord Chancellors against what looks like their policy in this respect. The fact is plain enough. There has indeed been some interest in the number of district judges conducting magistrates' courts in the past twenty five years or so. In context, this increase is not striking. The number, at a recent count, was around 150, while the number of justices of the peace was around 25,000. At the time of my appointment in 1989, there were around 30,000 justices . There are therefore fewer justices and rather more district judges. With the figures as they are, this seems little cause for concern. Until the 1960s the criminal work of magistrates' courts in inner London was entirely in the hands of metropolitan stipendiary magistrates. This is no longer the case, and lay magistrates now sit in inner London and discharge the same role. Here is a change in the other direction.

My own view of the recent history is that it is not relative numbers that are problematic, if anything is. A more strongly grounded cause of concern is the tendency for district judges to be assigned matters in which the public is likely to be interested. Any case which has attracted much public attention is likely to be dealt with by a district judge in its passage through a magistrates' court or its disposal there. While it will still be announced in the press and on news bulletins that, 'A man will appear before —

shire magistrates in the morning,' the subsequent hearing will now nearly always be taken by a district judge.

This development, which has attracted little or no comment, is quite recent. Few prosecutions can have attracted more public interest than that of Jeremy Thorpe MP, a former leader of the Liberal Party, in 1978. Thorpe was charged with conspiracy to kill Norman Scott, a one-time acquaintance, and with incitement to murder. At the time, the law provided for committal proceedings where the charges were indictable-only, as these charges were. Thorpe and his co-defendants therefore appeared before Minehead magistrates to be committed for trial or, if the bench were to be persuaded that there was no case to answer, to be discharged. Thorpe's solicitor, Sir David Napley, deals fully with what happened in his memoirs (*Not Without Prejudice*, 1982). He refers to 'the hearing of the proceedings before the Chairman of the Bench, a retired architect and wartime squadron leader, sitting with another professional man and a housewife'. I recall no suggestion in the public prints, once proceedings were over, that the Minehead bench, so composed, had proved inadequate to the task. What was required of it was nothing out of the ordinary for lay magistrates at that time. It amounted in large part to hearing advocates for the defendants question prosecution witnesses with a view to bringing out and testing their evidence. Only the length of the proceedings and the huge public interest were exceptional.

It is most improbable that such a task would now be assigned to a lay bench, and worth considering why this is so and whether the change has been necessary. The main – and perhaps sole – reason for it must be the apprehension that the justice presiding over a bench might be maladroit in his handling of proceedings, in particular in giving reasons for the bench's decisions. What may be of little significance in the course of routine business may seem to count for a lot when the gallery is crowded out with reporters. There is a real point here, but the effective freezing-out of the lay bench from handling cases in the public eye seems an exaggerated response. Here I must emphasise that I am concerned with only those cases. They are not especially likely to involve difficult points of law. Very little that comes to magistrates' courts does. There therefore seems no good reason why a lay bench should not dispose of them.

Cases which can be seen from the start to be legally complex are in current practice assigned to district judges and I am not suggesting that they should not be. Napley's account of the Thorpe case makes this distinction very clear. Here was a case of undoubted legal and procedural complexity. After the prosecution evidence had been presented, he and the legal representatives of the other persons charged submitted that there was no case to answer. He acknowledges that he did this with very little hope of success and in the event he did not succeed. A passing comment he makes is revealing: 'There was an exceedingly faint chance that an exceptionally strong and experienced stipendiary magistrate might have taken such a course [of refusing to commit], but it was realised from the onset that three lay magistrates would never do'. What he implies is that a main condition for the self-confidence needed to do something startling – and a refusal to commit in the Thorpe case would have been very startling – is the expert knowledge of a qualified lawyer. This may well be the case, and, insofar as he hints at a limitation of the capability of lay magistrates, I will consider it more fully below. One can grant such a limitation without at all granting that lay magistrates cannot be trusted to deal with matters involving the sons and daughters of TV personalities, famous footballers and the like.

In the summer of 2011 came a run of rioting and the ransacking of shops, even of arson, in urban areas of England. There were occasions when the police briefly lost, or were believed to have lost, control of the streets. In the following weeks, there were numerous arrests followed by appearances in court. The extra burden on the courts was considerable, and the response of those involved seems to have been found creditable. There were numerous extra sittings, many of which extended into the late evening or were held over the weekend. It is hard to be sure how the unexpected extra work was divided between district judges and lay magistrates, and anecdotal evidence is inconsistent. In a letter to *The Times* in the following January, a retired circuit judge recorded; 'It is their historic role as justices of the peace to maintain order promptly in their area and their handling of the inner-city disorder of last year has shown how effective they can be'. Other reminiscences of that period have however suggested that the district judges took a disproportionately large share of the work. If this was indeed the case, I can only say that it was unfortunate – at least from a partisan perspective. If lay magistrates are bad at responding adequately to unexpected demands, leaving this to their professional colleagues, they weaken their case against an increase in the number of these 'reinforcements'.

The Police

Few magistrates take much interest in their relationship with the police and even fewer of those sitting now are aware of the extent to which this has changed. For most of the nineteenth century, and for a long time before, the police worked under the general direction of the magistracy. In the special case of London, the control of the new metropolitan force, established in the 1820s, was assigned to the two justices of the peace appointed as commissioners. Even after the establishment of a modern system of local government in the late nineteenth century, the magistracy continued to be well represented on the bodies exercising control over the police within that system.

This is no longer the case. The day-to-day operations of the police have long been under their exclusive control. Policing is now seen as a specialism. It is now barely conceivable for the Metropolitan Police Commissioner or a chief constable to be anything other than a police officer of wide experience. Most people both take this for granted and, it can be assumed, approve. Executive and judicial functions are now held to be best managed and discharged apart.

This amounts to a rise in the standing of the police which has some large implications. For centuries, until little more than a century ago, the authority of the Crown and the government was represented in the counties by the Lord Lieutenant and the county magistrates, and in towns of any substance by the mayor and corporation. Anyone who inquired about that useful abstraction, 'the civil power', could be referred to these persons and bodies. They were visible, and might be somewhat frightening. This changed, slowly and incrementally over the course of the nineteenth century. At the start of that period, the civil power could draw for coercive support on a rudimentary constabulary of medieval origin and, in times of crisis, on the part-time soldiery at the disposal of the Lord Lieutenant. One such deployment of troops in St Peter's Fields outside Manchester, in 1819, is in all the history books. It was directed by the county magistrates for Lancashire, doing, no doubt, what they took to be their duty to maintain law and order. Subsequently, it came to be held widely that they had mistaken their duty and that their action was ill-judged and excessive. Hence the label, 'Peterloo' and the description 'massacre'. The sense that a better procedure had to be found for maintaining law and order must have been an early prompt to the long succession of changes, of which I have given some account above, which has taken from the magistracy all executive control of the police. In consequence, the identity of the civil power and its location is no longer so obvious.

The only plausible view of the matter seems to be that the civil power is now represented by the police. In extremity, the armed forces may be available in support, but it seems to be accepted that what this means is action in support of the police. What had been an instrument has now come to be regarded as an agent, even the prime agent. I am by no means saying that this is a simply undesirable development: it has some obvious advantages in point of the speed and co-ordination of police activity. However, I have to suggest that we have become accustomed to exercises of police powers which would have struck our tougher-minded ancestors as grossly overbearing.

So little is the enlargement of police powers a subject of concern that their extension by way of legislation usually passes without comment. One such is the almost total delegation to the police of powers of arrest. This has come about in stages, and only quite recently became complete. Until quite recently there was a statutory distinction of arrestable and non-arrestable offences. This distinction has now been ended, and – here I generalise – it may now be said that the police have discretion to arrest a supposed offender within the limits prescribed by the statute constituting the offence. It is no longer necessary is for the police to obtain an arrest warrant from a magistrate. If they act unreasonably or outside the prescribed limits, the person arrested may have a ground of action against them. This appears to be the only control or riposte, apart from the control which goes with the general supervisory power, until recently of police authorities, now of elected commissioners. I risk saying that there is a general sense among observers that this does not amount to much. Here is a plain case of an originally magisterial function passing elsewhere. It appears to be accepted by the public to the point of being taken for granted and I have rarely heard a magistrate complain or even remark on it. I have mentioned it here simply as evidence of the trend.

One exercise of police powers which has been controversial is 'kettling' – that is, containing a crowd and allowing no one in it to leave a marked-off area for hours at a time, even where his or her presence within it has been accidental. It is easy to see what can be achieved by measures such as this, and I must leave it to the reader to judge whether those benefits are sufficient to justify arbitrary detention, as it seems fair to call it. Certainly, it must now be taken as settled law that this is something the police can, in certain circumstances, do. In 2012 the European Court of Human Rights, endorsed this conclusion, bringing to an end proceedings brought by some persons 'kettled' in central London on 1 May 2001. The process of appeal was greatly drawn out, and it is at least encouraging to note that some people care enough about personal liberty to keep the argument going for so long.

I should make it clear that I am not suggesting any reinstatement of magisterial control over the police. There is a clear objection of principle to that, apart from obvious practical difficulties. What I am suggesting is that an inevitable change seems to have had some unwelcome consequences and that it would be as well to have those addressed. An imperfect system of lay control over the exercise of police powers has been dismantled, to be replaced not by a better one but, it seems, by one which amounts to a mere deficiency of control. It remains to be seen how the very recent establishment of elected police commissioners will bear on this.

Fixed-penalties

There are some other matters, closely related, with a bearing on the self-assurance and morale of the lay magistracy. One of these – the application of fixed-penalties – follows naturally from what has just been said about the powers of the police. Lay magistrates quite often voice concern over the fairly recent empowerment of police officers and some others to apply fixed-penalties – that is, to fine on the spot offenders who admit their offence. To be precise, offenders receive a notice and the money due is handed over later. This procedure was brought in, at first, to deal with offenders against road traffic law, but its scope has been extended. The concern voiced by many magistrates and others has been directed towards the procedure rather than towards the police, but the procedure involves the police so closely that the relationship must be affected to some degree.

It is easy to see the appeal of the fixed-penalty procedure. To the Government, it appeals because it is cheap and simple. A motorist concedes, let us say, that he is not wearing a seat-belt when he should be; he is given a notice to pay a fixed penalty at a court-house, the sum being well below the maximum permitted by statute; the law is thereby enforced and its enforcement should have some general deterrent effect; what the policeman does in such a case is just part of his job, and there is no extra cost there; the offender is relieved of the need to go to court and, in financial terms, gets off lightly. Here is the appeal to him too. The magistrates' courts are spared the addition to their lists of an item which is hardly contestable and where a Guilty plea is almost certain. The supposed offender has the right to decline to pay, leaving it to the police to prosecute him; in other words, he has his day in court if he wants it. What is there to be said against the procedure?

There are at least two objections of principle, though it is arguable how strong they are. One is that the employment of fixed-penalty notices amounts to an effective decriminalisation of a whole raft of offences, which are in effect downgraded and drained of the significance which should attach to breaches of the law. The fine is no longer seen as a penalty – that is, an expression of condemnation – but as no more than an extra cost. Something seems to be lost by this, which might be held to matter. Another principled objection is that with fixed-penalties there can be no matching of penalty to means: as they have to be invariable, they cannot be too high and there is therefore something of a bias in favour of the rich.

I must leave it to the reader to decide how much, if at all, these objections matter, when set against what seem to be the plain advantages of simplicity and economy offered by a fixed-penalty system. Most magistrates would, I think, object very little if fixed-penalties were to be applicable only in cases such as the one I have instanced, where the offence is decidedly minor. What has provoked much criticism is the tendency to extend their scope. There was much contention over this around the end of the last decade. Early in 2009, it was reported that the Justice Secretary at the time, Jack Straw, had been persuaded not to enlarge considerably the number of offences open to be disposed of in this way.

The Times of February 5, 2009, reported the reaction of the Chairman of The Magistrates' Association to this partial retreat:

> 'He welcomes Straw's decision to consult further. But JPs have won a battle, not the war, he says. "Serious offences must be brought to court and heard in public before properly selected and trained members of the judiciary." Justice, he accepted, must be administered expeditiously and some minor offences

are suitable for fixed penalties. But offences such as threats to destroy or damage property, or unacceptable behaviour on trains, could be serious. "It is crucial for the public to have an open and transparent justice system where victims and witnesses will have confidence that offenders are being dealt with appropriately."

These words chime in with other such declarations from magistrates of standing, to be found from time to time in the press. In a letter to *The Times* of September 3, 2008, the former chairman of a bench in the Greater Manchester area recorded a recent sharp decline in the work given to local magistrates. He referred to figures he had obtained from the local police which showed that 'fixed penalties are regularly being given for offences that would attract community penalties under the new sentencing guidelines including offences of theft and violence'. He went beyond bare complaint to suggest why such things happened, attributing them to the setting of targets for police officers: '... special priority payments for officers are now based on these targets. If the targets can be met by issuing a fixed penalty for a sanctioned detection then who can blame an officer for issuing that fixed penalty?'

What I have not seen pointed out – for all its oddity – is the way that this significant new development has come about after the effective ending of the control of the police by the magistracy. It is now agreed that the magistrate should not be anything like a super-policeman: the two functions should be kept quite separate. It therefore seems all the more remarkable that what we now see, if only on a limited scale, is the establishment of the policeman as something of a minor-magistrate in the powers available to him – more accurately, perhaps, as prosecutor and judge in one. It is not surprising that magistrates – not only lay magistrates – are concerned at this little-considered development, especially as it comes with the threat of more of its further extension. The perceptible note of self-interest in the way they register their concern is not surprising: they see their work being taken away and their place in the judicial scheme of things being made less significant. The case against fixed penalties is not to be disposed of simply by way of pointing this out.

Ministers and Public Opinion

Some tension between the public responsibility of those with an executive role, typically ministers, and those with the judicial role is inevitable. There will be occasions on which the public wants a strong response from ministers to some undisputed public evil, such as gross public disorder, the rioting and looting of the summer of 2011 being an instance of that. Ministers will want to respond as desired and part of their response is likely to be a call to the courts to act in a particular way, typically 'robustly' – that is, with unusual severity. A proper rejoinder to such a call from those charged with the judicial role would be that decisions on sentencing have been assigned to them, to be exercised in line with the guidance of the Sentencing Council and of the higher courts. The rejoinder is rarely heard. This may well be because it does not need to be made. Ministers should be able to voice public opinion and state their own view of what a particular crisis might require, without being supposed to believe that they can give instructions to those with a judicial role. Nonetheless, there is that in the relationship which I have called 'tension'. No stronger word is required, principally because both parties are too tactful to want a public argument. No doubt there is often no disagreement on substance: there seems to have been none in the summer of 2011. All concerned seem to have taken deterrent-sentencing to have been necessary.

It would, I think, be over-confident on the part of those with the judicial role, whether judges or magistrates, professional or lay, to trust that public opinion would be on their side in the event of any real disagreement. It is depressing to observe how frequently public opinion is over-excited by gross breaches of the law or well-publicised scandals. These outbursts of feeling are sometimes called 'moral panics'. They are usually by way of reaction to something widely publicised which clearly deserves to be taken seriously, though soberly. It is the perfervid nature of the reaction which is likely to disturb the sensitive. It is outside the scope of this book to consider this problem at length, and I will say only that one can imagine exceptional circumstances in which the lay magistracy, along with other judicial agents, might come to feel intimidated by public opinion; also that it is not out of the question that elected politicians – local perhaps, rather than national – might seek their own advantage in intervening. Here is what is certainly a threat, if (it now seems) a remote one.

Employed Persons?

I have touched above on the way in which the composition of the magistracy in point of social class has been transformed over the past century. This can now be seen as inevitable, and a concomitant of the transition to universal suffrage, though the growlings from 'Solicitor' in his appraisal of the magistracy of the interwar period suggest that not everyone found it a change for the better. The change is a main part of the move towards making the magistracy 'representative' in all respects. The desirability of this broader aim is now rarely questioned, though I will point out shortly what seem to me to be some of the disadvantages of over-emphasis.

'Representativeness' is too unfixed a notion for it to be easy to say how far it has been achieved – I would say largely so in most respects. The sexes are represented more or less equally. Political opinion is no longer an issue, as it was a hundred years ago, and the political allegiance of serving magistrates, so far as it becomes apparent, seems to be spread across the parties, at least in England and Wales taken as a whole. The young are under-represented, though this is inevitable as long as experience of life and evidence of some social service are taken to be relevant qualifications. Ethnic minorities are represented more or less in line with their proportion of the population as a whole. This leaves social class, where it can at least be said that the lay bench as a whole is not obviously unrepresentative of the population.

If this is so, then in at least one respect it may have come about at something of a price. A traditional argument for the lay magistracy was that it was independent, a large element in that independence being the enjoyment of independent means. Magistrates were unpaid and the threat of removal from the bench was at least not one of *financial* loss. Landowners, beneficed clergy, professional men of any standing and the employers of others on any scale were beyond intimidation. Those who were salaried were relatively few and, before 1900, wage-earners must have been very few indeed. Financial independence in itself is not however the main point. What may matter much more is the freedom from the habits, attitudes and presumptions that come from working for others and taking instructions.

From the perspective of a hundred years ago, what would, I fear, be most striking is the prevalence and dominance of just those habits, attitudes and presumptions and, in consequence, the diminution of the *manifest* independence which, on the traditional view, was one of the lay magistracy's greatest strengths. It is surely because so many magistrates are used to being employees that they have taken so readily to what is now required of them. Magistrates now seem to have become regulated to a high degree. They are

appointed through a process of interview, their performance on
the bench is appraised – if only, as yet, by their peers – they receive
training, some of it obligatory, and they may claim expenses. If lay
magistrates are not yet employees, they must often look as if they
are. The observers whom I imagined to be looking at the working
of a magistrates' court would surely have assumed this to be so.
Suppose our observer from the continent was French: he or she
would have found them to look and to act like *fonctionnaires*. He
or she would have been surprised to learn that they were unpaid,
having assumed, naturally enough, that no *fonctionnaire* would
work for nothing (The literal translation of this word, 'functionary',
seems all too happy). Is the non-payment of lay magistrates and
nothing more enough to sustain that independence?

A quite recent development seems to support this view of lay
magistrates as employees. It now seems to be established that a lay
magistrate who has been discomfited by some action of the officers
or other authorities of the local bench may start proceedings
before an employment tribunal with a view to having his grievance
remedied. This course of action at least appears to be available to
him only on the basis that a justice of the peace is an employed
person, even though he or she has no contract of employment
and receives no pay for services rendered. A different procedure
was already available. The High Court has always had jurisdiction
to review the administration of magistrates' courts and to correct
maladministration where a magistrate presented himself as
having suffered from it. In the 1990s, a London magistrate, who
claimed that he had been removed without good reason from
the category of those able to take the chair in court, sought this
remedy against the officers of his bench and their clerks, and was
successful in his application to the High Court.

It is easy to see why recourse to an employment tribunal has its
attractions. Recourse to the High Court is likely to be expensive.

It must be to the advantage of lay magistrates to have available to them a comparatively cheap and easy recourse when they are seriously aggrieved. What is worrying is that a change as substantial as this has been made – so far as one can tell – with very little consideration. It seems never to have been urged that the treatment accorded to a justice of the peace lay outside the jurisdiction of an employment tribunal. The respondents in cases taken to tribunals, who might have been expected to have made this point, if only on tactical grounds, seem not to have done so. It seems to have become accepted that recourse to a tribunal is available to lay magistrates. They must, it seems, count at least in some sense of the word as 'employed'. The implications of this, a conclusion reached almost casually, seem to be large.

It is hardly enough to point to district judges by way of suggesting that payment out of public funds, and the regulation likely to go with that, are not incompatible with judicial independence. Indeed they are not, but district judges have a stiffening in the form of a professional qualification – that of lawyers – which lay magistrates, with the odd exception, will continue to lack. I have referred to the concern which many magistrates expressed at the intention to turn their clerks into employees of the HMCTS. I recollect no such expression of concern on the part of magistrates over the status of magistrates themselves. Perhaps there should have been.

How it is Now

Over my last ten years on the bench, I sensed that morale among those serving had made some recovery. Few lay magistrates now expect their role and position to be done away with. The question of how it currently stands with their distinguished office has therefore become much less urgent. At the same time, they are likely to feel pressed upon from several sides at once. If they have nothing to complain about over their work, they can hardly fail to register the increase in the number of district judges and the tendency to assign to district judges all matters likely to attract much public attention. They are also likely to be aware of the acquisition by their clerks of functions once reserved to magistrates. Along with district judges they will have noted a decline in the volume of work and attributed this to the increased and increasing use of fixed-penalties.

There is one respect in which the standing of lay magistrates is now more secure, because more securely grounded, than it has ever been. The Lord Chief Justice is now the Head of the Judiciary and, in a loose sense, the judiciary is now taken to include the magistracy. The Lord Chancellor retains the 'ministerial' role – that is, he is responsible for appointing magistrates, but this is now done with the concurrence of the Lord Chief Justice, who is responsible for magistrates' welfare, training and deployment, and also for disciplinary action short of removal. Here is a barely perceptible but real enhancement of lay magistrates' status. The change seems to go with a recognition that more is now expected and required of them.

IS IT GOOD ENOUGH?

11.

Fit for Purpose?

The Morgan-Russell Report

I will now address directly the large question which has prompted me to write this book: is our system of summary justice good enough; how well does it work; is it fit for purpose? In one form or another, this question will have been apparent in much of the previous discussion and that discussion may have suggested an answer. I must now try to spell out that answer.

The lay magistracy is one element only within this system but, with its large numerical preponderance over district judges, it is of prime importance. I will therefore make it my first concern. It was around the turn of the century that the future of the lay magistracy was most obviously a subject of questioning and debate. The Chief Metropolitan Magistrate was in no position to address it directly on the occasion to which I have referred in the last chapter, but the Home Secretary of the time, Jack Straw, was widely believed to be inclined to favour the replacement of lay by stipendiary magistrates, whether in whole or in part. This belief will have been encouraged by the commissioning by his department and the Lord Chancellor's Department (those being the two then responsible), of a report bearing indirectly on the option of replacement. The report was entitled *The judiciary in the magistrates' courts*. I will refer to it as the Morgan-Russell Report after its principal authors.

The Report could hardly fail to be important, as it was the first comprehensive study of the efficiency of the lay magistracy since the Report of the Royal Commission of 1946/48 – efficiency, that is, in every sense. It resembles the Royal Commission's Report in being of consciously limited scope. The Royal Commission's Report was directly concerned only with justices of the peace. Morgan and Russell record that the research they conducted was commissioned to serve a rather different purpose. This was to:

> 'investigate the present balance of lay and stipendiary magistrates and the arguments supporting this balance;

> test the weight and validity of these arguments;

> consider whether each type of magistrate is deployed in the most effective way.'

Its collection of relevant statistics and its surveys of the opinions of those concerned with this part of the judicial system are highly informative. At the same time, the authors of the Report are well aware of this limitation of their, or any other pundit's, proper scope and power of analysis. In the section (1.3) headed 'The Research Remit' they comment:

> '... we should take this opportunity to emphasise what we do and what we do *not* take the term [quality] to mean and what we shall *not* be attempting to conclude in the report that follows. We were not in a position to assess the rectitude, appropriateness or justice of the decisions made by lay and stipendiary magistrates...'

This does not mean that no judgements of value were open to them:

'... we asked our court observers to apply the same sort of standards that magistrates apply to each other for appraisal purposes – for example, whether announcements are made in non-jargon language, easy for defendants and witnesses to understand and so on...'

I will pick out from the Report's conclusions those which are especially relevant. Stipendiaries were found to decide cases more quickly and so to handle more; they were also found to demonstrate a greater command over proceedings, pressing and challenging the advocates before them, no doubt with a self-assurance less commonly found in justices . This contrast, which is unsurprising, may not seem to matter all that much, as advantages may have their corresponding drawbacks – it is possible to be too self-assured – but there are other differences too striking to be shrugged off. The Report records that stipendiaries refused bail oftener, granted fewer adjournments – in 45% of applications against 52% granted by justices , and that in sentencing for 'either-way' offences they gave custodial sentences [for a first offence] to 25% of offenders against 12%.

Why was there so appreciable a difference in this last respect? Is there a tendency for district judges to be assigned cases where the offence is held – and, if so, by whom? – to be graver? If there is no such real difference, should it not be a pressing question which of the two constitutions of a magistrates' court is doing what should be done in such cases? I noted in Chapter One that it quite often happens that someone awaiting sentence by a lay bench is reassigned at little or no notice to a district judge – or *vice versa* – very probably just to even out the workload in two adjacent court-rooms, and for no graver reason. Should it not be worrying that such a reassignment – brought about by chance – more or less doubles or halves the chance of an offender going into custody? There is little awareness of this problem, if it is one. Among serving magistrates, of either category, I never heard it discussed.

The Report went beyond its authors' own observations to take account of the views of 'court-users', a category very largely made up of clerks, ushers, lawyers on each side and probation officers. Among court-users, the strengths just instanced were again attributed to stipendiaries, while lay magistrates were thought to have the advantage in the way they treated those before them, in being courteous, in using simple language and in showing concern. More generally, court-users were recorded as finding the differences between the two categories small. As for the general public, the Report noted that most people were unaware that there were two kinds of magistrates. When they were informed that there were, the presumptions recorded – which can have been no more than that – were that lay people would import the views of the community into the judicial process and would be more sympathetic to defendants' circumstances; also that stipendiaries would be more effective in determining verdicts. No one is likely to be surprised by these findings: the conclusion seems to be that the professionals have a decided edge, also that their possession of that edge is not an unqualified merit.

It is clear from the Report that Morgan and Russell found that the most plainly observable forms of effectiveness cannot be appraised in isolation. A typical stipendiary magistrate/district judge, they found, disposed of cases more promptly than the typical lay bench. Here is something plainly measurable, but the conclusions to be drawn are more in doubt. It may or may not be possible to establish how far the two forms of tribunal are dealing with the same sort of case. What is certainly more elusive is the impression this relative promptitude make on those so disposed of. How does it strike a broader public opinion, registered in the first place by the crowd in the gallery? Suppose this crowd, or the broader newspaper-reading public regard it, with approval, as evidence of professionalism? Suppose, on the other hand, it is registered as the outcome of a superficiality of approach, as a more-or-less automatic disposal of all too familiar business? Again, how much would it matter if it were found that this view of district judges' proceedings was widely held? How far should the public perception of the conduct of summary proceedings – assuming it could be established – be taken into account?

As for the cost-comparison, the Report observed that the *direct* cost of lay magistrates was greatly less than that of stipendiaries. When *indirect* costs were taken into account, the difference was very much less sharp. What counts as an indirect cost may be arguable: what certainly seems to count is the cost of support-staff employed at court-houses, especially that of legally qualified clerks, the cost of maintaining buildings, and an apportionment of the cost of the staff of the Ministry of Justice (as it now is) and of advisory committees. A cost-comparison is therefore not straightforward. Furthermore, it may be rash to assume that if more district judges were to be appointed, they would deliver justice in just the same way as the relatively few now in post. Would they continue to pass more custodial sentences than their remaining lay colleagues? If so, should the extra burden on the prison service be taken into account? If it should, the point is not one of cost only, but also one for evaluation. Is prison the best disposal for roughly a quarter of offenders in this category, against roughly one eighth? If we take the comparison in this respect to be in the stipendiaries' favour, it may be judged to be worth having, even at a higher cost. If not, not.

Two conclusions, both modest ones, are prompted by study of the Morgan-Russell Report. One is that there is nothing in its analysis and findings to suggest that lay justice, as it now is, is not at least passable and adequate and much to suggest that it is at least broadly acceptable to an admittedly poorly informed public opinion. The other is that the cost-comparison with the obvious alternative is not easily made and, as made in the Report, hardly conclusive.

My Own Observations

In what follows, I will draw largely on my own experience and will go along with the authors of the Report in offering an appraisal which is limited in its scope to what is observable. I say limitation, and not exclusion, as it is certainly no proper aim to lose sight altogether of the ideal of substantive justice – that is, 'rectitude, appropriateness ' and so on. The plain question, 'Do the courts get it right?, is a very good one as well as being one that is inevitable. The question is complex as well as plain and, as commonly put, certainly extends to the sound determination of evidence and to proper sentencing. My observations are founded on my own experience and on no professional expertise comparable to that behind the Morgan-Russell Report. I have of course discussed them with others and doubt if many of those with comparable experience – fellow magistrates, legal advisors, lawyers familiar with magistrates' courts – would be altogether out of sympathy with what follows.

DAMNING

I will start with the impartiality of lay magistrates, with their freedom, or lack of it, from bias. This would be hard to appraise through court-observation, as that would expose bias only in its grosser forms. Attempts to appraise it through analysis of statistics are sometimes made but, to the best of my own judgement, have been inconclusive. I can therefore record only my own impression, for all its obvious limitations. This is that it is a strong point in favour of lay justice, as it now operates, that the necessary impartiality has been achieved. In twenty years service I observed almost nothing in my fellow justices to suggest that they had been or would be influenced, in a way that would impair justice, by a private sympathy or antipathy. It is this, I am assuming, what we are concerned with when we talk of 'prejudice', a word which it is not easy to define (Most obviously, if we know what our prejudices are, are they to be called prejudices? In common usage, the word seems to denote *unconscious* bias?). If my perception was sound, the selection-process for lay magistrates has in this respect at least functioned well. It may be said that what I observed was people on their best behaviour, careful perhaps to conceal their sympathies and antipathies for the brief period of a day in court. This may indeed have been the case, and it seems to me to matter little if it were, as the resolve to conceal goes with the recognition of what needs to be concealed. Such recognition should be enough to diminish the risk. It would be hard to devise a procedure for selection up to picking out for rejection the clever applicant well aware of his antipathies, able to coved them up and resolved to act on them. But I never came across anyone on the bench whom I took to be such a person.

I am confined to the limits of my own observation quite as much when I deal with the judicial and intellectual quality of those justices – some hundred and fifty or so over a twenty-year period – with whom I served. Along with freedom from bias and prejudice, this is what any selection-process must be concerned with, and for what it is worth my observation was that in this respect the process was notably less successful.

The bench on which I served varied in size between some seventy and some ninety over the period of my membership. At any one point within this period about half a dozen of my colleagues, maybe more, seemed to me to be first-rate: as efficient as a good stipendiary magistrate/ district judge in every respect except in knowledge of the criminal law and sometimes, as far as I could judge, little behind even there. There were also about half a dozen who in my judgement, shared (so far as I could make out) by the bulk of the bench, should never have been appointed. The deficiency was in almost every case one of intellectual capacity or training, manifest in failure to grasp the point at issue, to see what worked as an argument and what did not. I recall the colleague who, over the course of a trial, took few or no notes of the evidence and who, in the retiring room, seemed to rely on her intuition to tell who was truthful and who was not. Usually, in these rare cases, the simple truth was that one of one's colleagues was just not very clever; sometimes it seemed more likely that what was lacking was anything like intellectual training.

How much this mattered in practice is not easy to say. It must have been only infrequently that two justices of this level of competence sat together and, even when that happened, neither would have taken the chair. The procedure for selecting chair-takers could be relied on in this respect. Incompetence would not have been on public view, as it might have been in the past, but evident only in the retiring room. Most people are more or less aware of their limits and I found that the few plainly inadequate magistrates generally deferred with little fuss to their colleagues, certainly if those colleagues were sufficiently assertive. That such an outcome was unsatisfactory hardly needs to be said, but unsatisfactory does not usually mean disastrous. It must be decidedly rare for substantive injustice to come about through the purely intellectual inadequacy of one out of three of those delivering it. Nonetheless, unsatisfactory it is.

With these qualifications I agree with the Morgan-Russell Report that summary justice as it now is, with its lay preponderance, is at least not so inadequate that it cannot be allowed to pass. It is, in the strict sense of the word, acceptable. That there is little public interest in it, though attributable in part to a mere lack of public knowledge, is a factor which favours its continuance. Such awareness as there is probably goes little further than appreciation that there is some lay participation in the criminal justice system and approval of that. Here one can only speculate. I believe that a complete supersession of the lay magistracy by professional lawyers would be decidedly unpopular, especially if it threatened to be expensive. There is an unfocused, and commonly unvoiced, public feeling in favour of the jury-system – which tends to become vociferous whenever there is talk of limiting the right to jury trial. It may well be that something of the same sentiment attaches to the lay magistracy. It is a feeling that this sensitive area of life should not be left entirely to professionals.

The Conditions for Improvement

In the next two chapters, I will consider how the performance of the lay magistracy might be made more effective, having, I trust, said more than enough to bring out the need for enhanced effectiveness. I will not go more widely than this to consider how the process of criminal justice as a whole needs to be made more efficient. My prime concern in this book has been more narrow, directed to those charged with delivering justice. Here, I will try to indicate some changes for the better. For this, two conditions need to be are satisfied.

The first is that there should be sufficient resolution on the part of those responsible – that is, in the first place, ministers and, in the second, those charged with directing the Courts Service – that the lay magistracy should retain a central role. This means that its field of work should not come to be confined to a residual category of business, of a kind which is held not to need the attention of a district judge. A slide towards this is probably already under way. I have dealt above with one sign of it, the tendency for anything which has attracted public attention to be assigned to a district judge. This tendency needs to be checked, as such business only rarely raises points of any legal complexity. It has to be attributed to an apprehension that lay magistrates would not be up to doing the job in a way that would satisfy the public and withstand close scrutiny in the press. If there is any basis for this apprehension, which I doubt, it should be addressed by way of training and pre-trial preparation. If it were ever to become the general perception that the work of justices was confined to a residual category of the undemanding, the effect on recruitment to the bench would be bad. Here is something for the attention of the powers that be.

The second pre-condition for improvement is the retention of the present 'adversarial' system of criminal justice, with its focus on proof. This may seem hardly worth mentioning here, as it is rare to come across any worked-out proposal for its replacement, but there is enough growling from the sides to make it necessary to touch on the question. The 'adversarial' system needs to be retained if the lay magistracy is to be retained, simply because it is comparatively simple to operate: when the charge is disputed and there is a trial, the tribunal – here a bench of three justices – has the straightforward task of deciding whether the prosecution case has been made out, and made out to the high standard of 'being sure' or 'beyond reasonable doubt'. It is usually not too difficult to decide on that: the task is a lot easier than that of forming a firm view of 'what happened'.

Proponents of moving to an 'inquisitorial' system are rarely historians, and so commonly fail to make the obvious point that such a move would represent a qualified return to the way the process was conducted before the great enlargement of the role of the criminal defender over the course of the eighteenth century. My account of this development in Chapter Eight should have shown that criminal justice in the English tradition has not always been 'adversarial' in process. This may indeed suggest that there is a case for change which is rarely put forward. What we find instead is the expression of unfocused discontent, usually going with some animus against lawyers. In Chapter Seven, I quoted from a letter to *The Times* by Austen Mitchell MP. Later in that letter, after denouncing 'game-playing', he seems to be calling for magistrates to resume an inquisatorial role:

> 'So the magistracy must acquire the skills and the confidence it needs when defendants are not represented. Courts should not have to depend on the lawyers or wait for the evidence to be served up on a plate'.

On the face of it, what he seems to advocate would accommodate lay magistrates rather well, given their possession, often claimed for them, of the plain man's 'common sense' and sense of fairness. Doubts come in when one reflects on the procedure which such a re-jigged court would need to adopt, where there was no admission of guilt from the person charged. Whether lay magistrates would be up to the 'inquisitorial' function of getting at what happened is doubtful, to say the least. This is not easy: probing questioning, pressed home, is a technique to be learned, and it requires a certain flair. It is only those with at least the germ of that ability who should be advised to go to the Bar. Justices of the peace had this role in the distant past but we have almost no evidence how well they discharged it.

My own experience of service on the bench chimes in with the conclusion of the Morgan-Russell Report that the administration of justice by lay magistrates, as it now operates is at least adequate. It is passably effective, despite some unfavourable comparisons with district judges, balanced by some, though fewer, comparisons in lay magistrates' favour. The present way of doing things therefore seems good for at least a few more years. Its persistence depends, in my view, on the maintenance of the present 'adversarial' system of criminal justice, but this seems to be a safe assumption, given the feebleness and infrequency of calls to depart from it. It may however be urged that passable effectiveness is not enough, amounting to an over-willingness to be content with the second-best. I will therefore not conclude at this point but consider next how things might be improved.

12.

Making it Better

The Process of Appointment

Selection for appointment to the magistracy is of prime importance. Appointment remains the responsibility of the Lord Chancellor, though it now requires the concurrence of the Lord Chief Justice. In practice, the business of selection continues to be delegated to the advisory committees set up in 1910.

I have already given some account of how I came to be selected. The procedure under which the committees operate is more elaborate than it was, and there are now two interviews. The form which referees are asked to complete is decidedly more probing than such forms commonly are. As for the advisory committees' own composition, applicants for membership who are themselves serving magistrates will be interviewed by panels largely composed of present or outgoing members of the committee. This has the advantage of giving the task to people well used to personnel-selection, and who should be good at it, also to those who know what useful membership of an advisory committee requires. It may however have the balancing disadvantage that the composition of the committees becomes over-standardised: like might come too easily to appoint like. It is hard to say how far this has come to be the case.

What of the outcome? How far are the right people and only the right people appointed lay magistrates? In one respect, the present procedure seems to work well: it is decidedly unusual for a lay magistrate to be removed for misconduct. What is harder to calculate is the number of those resigning to avoid removal; there must be some and their number may well be higher. Even taking the two together, those departing must make up a very small percentage of the total of around 25,000 lay magistrates.

Much more numerous than those who certainly need to go or to be removed are those, sometimes of long standing, who may be perfectly honest and personally amiable, yet whose judicial and other intellectual qualities are plainly inadequate. I have already recorded that my bench always had a few such members. There was a general agreement among the majority who they were, though this was rarely voiced. I took this reticence to come from a mixture of decent tact and helplessness. It is not easy to see what can be done in such cases, as the obvious course, that of removal, would have strong countervailing disadvantages.

I take it to be essential that those appointed to a judicial role – and this extends to magistrates – should be secure in that position. This is not accepted universally, as is sometimes evident when a judge (as it usually is) passes a sentence which an excited public opinion finds surprising. In a case of homicide or rape, for instance, the offender may be treated with surprising leniency, the judge having found the offence or the offender – or both – to call for an exceptional course. Such a decision often produces howls of protest and calls for the judge to be removed from office. These howls will be disregarded, which is quite as it should be. Anyone dispensing justice should be supported without reserve when the ground of complaint is no more than a decision which has jarred with popular sentiment.

It may be urged that this principle, however sound in its way, should not apply to judicial agents who for whatever reason perform badly, and who seem beyond improvement. Why should such judges or magistrates not be open to removal, as they might be in other spheres of employment? In the case of lay magistrates, it may be urged that removal would be all the less problematic as they would not suffer any loss of income. There is some force in this, but I find it, finally, unpersuasive. The security in office of judicial agents is so highly desirable that it is necessary to endure some incidental deficiencies and discomforts. The barrier against removal has to be high. If it were to be lowered, it would be easy to slide towards accepting that magistrates unpopular with their colleagues or with the officers of their bench should for that reason only be required to go.

This makes it all the more important to ensure that only those who will do the work well should be appointed. This object is indeed largely achieved. The plain failures of the appointment-process are few, and it may be that this is the best that can be hoped for. Selecting people for jobs is not easy and no procedure for doing it will deliver complete success. This is certainly so, but it does not follow that there need be no change at all. I will now consider some respects in which the appointment-procedure might be improved.

'Representative'

The appointment of lay magistrates is dealt with comprehensively in the Lord Chancellor's and Secretary of State's Directions for Advisory Committees on Justices of the Peace. The title of this document makes it plain where the Directions come from, and so what authority they have. Such a document is bound to be open to up-dating: I will refer to, and quote from, the edition effective during my time on the bench.

What is said in the Directions about appointment will surprise no one. In considering applications, the committees are to look for six 'key qualities': good character; understanding and communication; social awareness; maturity and sound temperament; sound judgement; and commitment and reliability. Each of these receives some elaboration. This emphasis is no doubt grounded in long collective experience of the discharge of a magistrate's role. No one is likely to quarrel with it.

The Directions are of much interest for what they do not say. I have dealt in Chapter Eight with the changes which followed the long-postponed Liberal victory in the general election of 1906 and the establishment of a Royal Commission which reported in 1910. This led to the effective delegation of magisterial appointments to the advisory committees then brought into being. It is hard to say how far things were changed by the new mode of appointment and how far by the abolition of the property qualification for the magistracy around the same time. The two changes had the same rationale, that the magistracy should be 'representative' in its composition. This needs to be made clear, as that concern is not to be dismissed as no more than a recent instance of what is often called, usually derisively, 'political correctness'. It is at least a hundred years old and has been favoured on all sides. Something like it was strongly favoured by Lord Hailsham. In the memoirs to which I have referred, he wrote:

'By far the most important factor a Lord Chancellor has to examine in making appointments to a Bench is social and political balance. In some parts of the country it is only too easy to get benches consisting of nominations in themselves perfectly suitable but, coming as a whole from one class or one political party, to the exclusion of all others... The search for young blood, magistrates from minority groups, and women suitable and willing to serve is almost continuous, and the newer parties always tend to be under-represented.'

Anyone who keeps abreast of public debate will know that Hailsham's concern of forty years ago is so widely felt as to be part of a common moral orthodoxy. The point he makes is often heard, usually more loudly. It is therefore noteworthy that the Directions give the advisory committees no unequivocal steer towards seeking diversity in their recommendations, in whatever form or to whatever degree. The one point where there is a clear declaration of intention is to be found in what is said about the issue of letters from an advisory committee conveying its decision not to recommend someone. The committees are told not to give concern for diversity as a reason for their decision. To quote from the Directions (para. 3.6.9):

'In giving detailed reasons [to unsuccessful candidates] letters must *not* make mention of bench-balancing factors, as these must *not* be used in the process.' (emphasis in original)

The Directions make little use of the italics of emphasis; their appearance here suggests that the point is both important and difficult.

At the same time, among the returns which the advisory committees are charged with making is a form which requires them to break down their recommendations in respect – among other things – of age and ethnicity (whether or not BME, 'black and minority ethnic). Here is a decided oddness: the committees are not to seek a particular outcome in respect of diversity – quite the opposite – but they are required to report how far that outcome has been achieved or – to put it neutrally – how far it has come about.

Degrees of 'Representativeness'

'Representativeness' or 'diversity' is not a simple notion. It can take various forms and be found in different degrees. The most useful categorisation of these forms and degrees is, I believe, one which distinguishes 'the weak', 'the strong' and 'the stronger-still'. The difference between the three lies in the extent to which the principle to be applied is taken to be over-riding, to be so important that other considerations should give way.

On the 'weak' form, the object should be to ensure that no one suitable for appointment should be ruled out on grounds of race or class, or other irrelevant ground such as sexuality. On the 'weak' form, this is all that should be ensured. Supporting arguments for this position may seem hardly necessary, as it rarely comes under attack, but an obvious one is the need to avoid the considerable social resentment that would follow from the advisory committees or some comparable bodies acting in what would seem a prejudiced way. Another, no less obvious, and for most of us decisive, is that people qualified to sit as lay magistrates are not so easily found that any field of recruitment can safely be disregarded or people coming from it viewed unfavourably for no good reason. Both these considerations seem strong, and few people – and I am not one of them – would now object to the representative principle in the 'weak' or basic form.

On the 'strong' form, appointment would continue to be made on merit or suitability, whatever the criteria for those qualities should be taken to be. It would however be a main object to bring into being a magistracy which, in respect of race, class, or other such categorisation, was a cross-section of the whole population. On this basis, it would be legitimate to discriminate in favour of under-represented groups, but only to the extent of favouring them in cases where suitability for appointment, on all other grounds, was equal.

The 'stronger-still' form would go beyond this in favouring those from under-represented groups even over better-qualified applicants from over-represented groups, on condition that those to be favoured in this way had at least reached the basic acceptable standard. It will be evident that those who favour the 'stronger still' approach take representativeness to be so important that that it should outweigh, in importance, the object of having the best possible lay magistracy. I leave aside – for the moment – the question of what the 'best possible' magistracy would be. It is this form of the representative principle that appears now to be favoured.

Hailsham's concern seems to have been that a main condition of the acceptability of the lay magistracy to the population as a whole was a fair degree of representativeness, which would be recognised as such. He seems to have supposed that a less than fully expert – because unprofessional – magistracy would have a compensating strength, one which the fully professional alternative would inevitably lack. This would make up, or more than make up, for any deficiency in expertise. How far he would have pressed this line of argument is unclear. The words I have quoted seem to suggest that he would have been prepared to go beyond the 'weak' form in seeking to achieve his object. The Morgan-Russell Report, coming from a different angle, says something comparable:

> 'Not only is the office of Justice of the Peace ancient and in an important tradition of voluntary public service, it is also a direct manifestation of government policy which encourages *active citizens* in an *active community*. In no other jurisdiction does the criminal court system depend so heavily on such voluntary unpaid effort.' (emphasis in original)

In other words, the benefits of lay justice can be felt in spheres well removed from the purely judicial. The argument seems to depend largely on the citizens being of all kinds, to the extent perhaps of being a cross-section of the community.

A rather narrower argument is also commonly pressed. This is that the magistracy will only be acceptable to elements within the population if those elements are represented in it in the same rough proportions. By 'acceptable' is usually meant 'credited with understanding' or 'found trustworthy'. It is argued that, if I am an X, I can only be fully confident of getting a fair – and comprehending and courteous – hearing if others in the class of X are involved in dealing with me. There is an obvious difficulty with this. The minority group X might be represented proportionally in the lay magistracy as a whole, nation-wide, but yet under-represented on the local bench which will be dealing with me. Even when it has its 'proper' representation on the local bench, the three persons before whom I appear may be – very likely will not be – none of them X.

It may be that the importance of having at least one X as a member of any tribunal dealing with members, or a single member, of class X is such that the constitution of the tribunal should be manipulated to ensure it. I have heard this proposed or at least claimed to be desirable. For my own part, I find it both dubious in principle and impracticable. Magistrates should be selected for their possession, among other things, of an ability to deal fairly and with understanding with all who appear before them. For this, they require a fair knowledge of life and some imaginative sympathy. Their work on the bench will serve well to develop those qualities, if only they are present at least in germ from the start. The 'average' magistrate will not have the direct experience of being X but should be able to enter into that experience, at least to a fair degree, by way of empathy.

As for what is achievable in practice, there might be enough Xs on a local bench to constitute a tribunal containing at least one of them whenever the defendant was an X. This would not however be enough for full assurance. Any arrangement for a X to sit on a particular occasion would be insecure. It would be liable to collapse whenever one of those rostered needed to exchange an allocated sitting or whenever it became necessary to move the X-case to another courtroom, as is often necessary to redistribute workload. Advocates of the 'stronger-still' view who were prepared to go to an extreme might indeed argue that an X-case should never be dealt with without an X on the bench. Call that the 'strongest-possible' view No one with any acquaintance with the day-to-day administration of a courthouse is likely to take that to be feasible. The most that might be brought about by the 'strong' version and its 'stronger' variants would be making it more *likely* that defendant X will be dealt with by a bench containing at least one X. Is this strictly limited success worth the elaboration and distortion of procedures that would be need to bring it about?

It will be apparent that I take the benefits of the 'stronger-still' version to be outweighed by the plain disadvantage which comes with it – that is, the appointment to the bench, not only of those judged to be best qualified to serve but also of some judged to be adequate – but no more – and whose appointment would contribute more effectively to representativeness. I have given reasons for supposing that this is not an object worth pursuing at the price which would have to be paid, especially as it would never be more than imperfectly achieved. The same considerations should rule out the 'strong' version, even if that is much less open to objection. The short point is that all that criminal justice requires is a fair trial before persons sufficiently equipped by intellect, character, sense of values and due preparation to provide one. This all that defendants and other participants can reasonably expect or hope for. To go beyond that and to specify that a due proportion of those persons should be of the same category of humanity as oneself is to require too much. Making any form of representativeness other than the 'weak' form a prime object therefore seems ill-judged.

It may seem to have been unnecessary to have pressed the argument as far as I have, given that the Directions state that bench-balancing should be no part of an advisory committee's discharge of its task even if – as we have seen – it should be part of its concern, at least in the making of reports. It has seemed necessary because of the widespread belief that, whatever the Directions said, the committees have for some time done what they are told not to do and set such store by diversity that they are ready to operate on the basis of the 'stronger-still' basis, as I have called it. This means that they will on occasion prefer applicants in an 'under-represented' category over those in categories well represented on the bench. It follows that they will sometimes have appointed candidates whom they have found adequate, and no more than adequate, rather than others whom they have judged to be much more than adequate. It would be agreeable to suppose that the widespread belief was mistaken, or at least that the committees no longer proceed in such a way, as it must have been likely that the reputed procedure resulted in appointments which were weak absolutely. No system of appointment will be secure against this outcome; appointing people to jobs is not an easy business. My own experience – and here it can be no more than that – is that a concern for representativeness going beyond the 'weak' form must be in part responsible for the few plainly poor appointments.

Positive Discrimination – Attitude

I have so far been criticising the form of positive discrimination presently practised, that is in favour of groups marked out by race or class held to be under-represented. There are other forms of discrimination for which a case might be made and which are therefore worth discussing here. One such bears on the view of the objects of sentencing taken by candidates for appointment. This is something which almost inevitably comes up during the appointment-process. At present, discussion at interviews seems to be on the basis that there is a wide diversity of view on the proper objects of sentencing and that this diversity will be and should be reflected on the bench. It hardly needs saying that if representativeness is of prime importance that will be the only possible basis. On that criterion, if there is no consensus in society over what sentencing is for and what it should achieve there will be, and should be, the same diversity of view on the bench. That is how it is now. In consequence, magistrates differ, sometimes sharply, over the objectives of their sentencing. I have given examples of such disagreement in earlier chapters. I recall occasions where – when a custodial sentence was in question – there was the objection, 'But that won't do him any good,' where this was countered by the claim that the object was to punish the offender and deter others. On such occasions, the question whether or not to send the offender down would be resolved by the position taken or bias – if that is the proper word – of the third member of the bench.

This representation of all positions on sentencing naturally results in inconsistency of outcome. Inconsistency cannot be fully avoided, but it might in time be minimised if the attitudes and – finally – values of candidates for appointment were to be probed. This might be done by making inquiries of referees and by questioning at interviews which would need to be more systematic than it is at present. One can at least imagine a common view on the objects of sentencing developing among legislators and coming to modify the present general view, reflected in statute which, as I have shown, admits a range of objects. If this ceased to be an object of party-political contention and came to be taken for granted, would it not make sense to see that, as far as possible, no one would be appointed to the bench without broadly subscribing to it? If this were to come about, there could be something like a common policy in the sphere of criminal justice. At present there is no such statement of policy beyond what is expressed in the very general statement of the objects of sentencing in the Criminal Justice Act of 2003. It is easy to see the advantages of having one, and of having judicial agents, including magistrates, who would have a broad commitment to it.

Unhappily or not, this outcome is hardly attainable. Its achievement would require a general concurrence on what the policy should be and the maintenance of that concurrence over a period. This is not easy to envisage. It would require the quizzing of applicants for appointment over their views on the objects of sentencing. This would have to be of a much more thorough kind than that presently employed, as it would amount to testing their subscription to a moral orthodoxy. How candid would the responses of those questioned be, once it came to be appreciated that this was so? When the concern was with political balance on the bench, magistrates were regularly asked how they habitually voted. It seems safe to assume that nearly all of the answers given to this question were truthful. On that assumption, the inquiry would have produced clear-cut and relevant information, for instance that such-and-such a proportion of serving magistrates in a specified area was Labour-supporting. Action could then have been taken to redress an excess or deficiency. Imagine the comparative uselessness of asking magistrates or candidates for appointment whether or not their approach to sentencing was 'retributivist'. Here is a term open to being taken several ways; should those also be spelled out, and could the spelling out be done in a neutral and uncontentious way?

Any attempt to bring into being a magistracy of one mind on controversial points would, I believe, be hopeless. The likely public reaction to such an attempt, once it became evident, would not be favourable. It goes without saying that the diversity of opinion in the population on controversial matters is to be found at least as much on points of penological principle as on others. To the extent that the magistracy is successfully representative, that diversity will be found there. The price of this is that the object of pursuing a common policy on crime, an elusive purpose anyway, finds in this diversity of opinion a further handicap. It is yet one more obstacle in the way of a Lord Chancellor/ Justice Secretary concerned to set out and press home such a policy. This has to be endured.

Positive Discrimination – Intellectual Capacity

The advisory committees are directed to look for particular qualities and qualifications in making their recommendations. One quality notably absent from the list is intellectual power. My own experience is that it is deficiency in this respect which is the most obvious characteristic of the few plainly inadequate magistrates. If you are not very clever, you will either be ignored, with some embarrassment, as discussion in the retiring room becomes vigorous, or you will be a cypher, agreeing without understanding with the most combative of your colleagues. On one occasion, in the Crown Court, where we were hearing appeals, I heard my lay colleague, a woman from my own bench, assure the circuit judge who was in the chair that she agreed with him. This sounded all very well, but at that point in our proceedings the judge had yet to state a view. Magistrates who are not quick-witted, and who know it, tend to be much too deferential. The deference is as often as not accorded their legal advisors, a weakness which

'Solicitor' pointed out some eighty years ago. It is best to put the point with some bluntness: you need to be quite clever to be an effective lay magistrate.

It would not be difficult to skew the appointment-process accordingly. Intellectual capacity is not difficult to assess by means of interview. Anyone with the right experience can turn discussion into fields where the intellectual 'horse-power' and the degree of intellectual training of the person being interviewed will normally become apparent. Other desirable qualities may be hard to discover this way, but these are not.

One way of setting the intellectual standard required of those to be appointed would be by reference to an outside comparison. It might be declared that, though lay magistrates do not need a professional qualification to sit, they should be of the calibre to have been capable of acquiring one. They do not need to be solicitors, for example, but they should be people who could have become such if their ambitions had turned that way.

The advantages of introducing such a requirement seem obvious. What might be said against it? The usual objection is that it would represent a devaluation of the commonsense and experience of life now often strongly pressed as qualifications. It is hard to weigh up this objection, as it can only rest on general observation. I can see no reason why the admittedly desirable qualities which it holds up should not be found in people up to gaining a professional qualification. In other words, my general observation differs from that of those advancing the objection. The point is hardly arguable.

The difficulty is practical. It is that the field of recruitment would be so far narrowed if the criteria for appointment were to be made more stringent in this way that it would no longer be possible to make the number of new appointments necessary. It is difficult to calculate how far this would be the case, but I have to concede that I find the objection plausible. If the qualifications for service on the lay bench are set too high, it will become impossible to man it.

I must now sum up. I agree that it is plainly right to ensure that no one otherwise well qualified to serve on the bench should be ruled out from doing so by some irrelevant characteristic, whether of sex, ethnic background, sexual orientation or whatever. Beyond this, I believe it to be either unnecessary or impracticable to go. It seems likely that attempts to go further will have done harm rather than good in leading to some embarrassingly weak appointments. Here, I would point to the way the application over the past century of what I am advocating here has been quite enough to remove two kinds of imbalance, those of sex and politics. There are now roughly equal numbers of men and women on the lay bench and it is no longer thought necessary to question serving and aspirant magistrates over their politics. Some problems solve themselves, with the application over a long term of procedures free from bias.

Training – If We Call it That

The training offered to – or obligatory for – lay magistrates is a much less contentious topic. I have already dealt with the instruction and discussion laid on, principally by the staff of the court service, and normally by the legal advisors who sit with magistrates in court, but also by The Magistrates' Association by way of addresses delivered at its regular meetings. The usefulness of this and the quality of its presentation are inevitably highly variable, but my experience is that what is offered – on the whole, more or less competently – makes lay magistrates more effective. It is hard to see how they would have been able to accommodate the changes introduced by successive and quite frequent Criminal Justice Acts without such support. All I have to propose, therefore, is more of the same. The Morgan-Russell Report picked up some respects in which lay magistrates were less effective than district judges, notably managing cases and dealing firmly enough with advocates. My own experience leaves me in no doubt that this was a telling observation. Pondering my own performance in the chair after a sitting, there were respects in which I often found myself rating it critically. It will of course always be much easier for a one-time practising advocate, now a district judge, to manage cases and to deal fairly and firmly with the lawyers appearing before him. It should however be possible to make the contrast between the professional and the lay magistrate less sharp, and this should become an immediate object of the training offered.

Something should be said about the word 'training' and its overtones. When something of the sort was brought in for judges, the word was avoided – I believe at the wish of those who were to receive what would be offered. Certainly, the responsible body was styled The Judicial Studies Board. It is now called The Judicial College. Nomenclature remains important. What is unhappy about talk of 'training' in this context is that it suggests simply the conveying of information and its absorption: the recipient takes in what is put to him or her, or comes to practise some skill until performance is up to standard. Everyone will at some time have needed training: learning how to use a computer will be a recent instance for many of us, no easy acquisition without straightforward instruction: 'this is how you do that', 'don't do that on any account'. Training is certainly necessary, and it may be that magistrates need more of it. My reservation is by way of recalling the distinction between training and education. Here is a common and, I hope, simple and obvious distinction: training is about the acquisition of skills, while education is about the development of the mind. Nearly all of us need both, if not at the same time; and the latter should not be reduced to the former.

The question can then be seen to be whether what lay magistrates require is analogous to training or to education or, if both, in what combination. My point is that in calling all that is offered 'training' there is a risk of importing an undesirable narrowness of approach. The point can be put more broadly. Training seems to involve the turning out of its recipient as a performer, one whose performance comes up to a specification. In this, there seems to be an inescapable presumption of subordination on the part of the recipient, here the lay magistrate, in his or relation to the instructor, as often as not one of the clerks who advises justices in court. This unfortunate presumption is likely to reinforce the other impairments of the lay magistrate's status with which I have already dealt (see Chapter Ten). It fits all too easily with a view of the lay magistrate as an employee, one who does what he is told.

Let me make it clear that I am not denying that within this sphere some, indeed much, activity is required which can only be called training. What I take to be needed is a broader conception under which training is only a part of what lay magistrates are offered. A term which reflects such a conception is needed, if not immediately obvious. 'Education' and 'Studies' would be as misleading as 'Training', if in the opposite way. The happiest term would, I believe, be 'Briefing', as this would reflect the submissions of civil servants to ministers, documents usually conveying much plain information and concluding with advice, but without the implication that the recipient minister must do what he or she is told. Changing the word used would, I believe, be helpful, though it would not go very far without a developing recognition that the lay magistrate is not a *fonctionnaire*. This is not a point on which it is easy to be optimistic.

In sum, therefore, I believe that the changes I have just set out as desirable, in respect of both selection and training, would in the medium term produce a more effective lay magistracy. It will be observed that they are far from radical. This moderation hardly needs defending, as I believe it accords broadly with popular sentiment, which is generally accepting of the lay magistracy where it is not merely unconcerned. It also has the broad backing of the most recent systematic survey of the field, the Morgan-Russell Report. There is however an arguable case for more radical change, and I consider this in my next and concluding chapter.

Should Lay Magistrates Be Paid?

If lay magistrates have all the usual attributes of employed persons other than that of being paid, their not being paid may seem anomalous; why should they not be? Non-payment is hardly a point of principle, as the first justices , those of the fourteenth century, received payment, though this seems to have been intended only to cover their costs – to be expenses, as we would say. It seems probable that this arrangement ceased once the sums paid over had come to seem trivial. Apart from this, justices were formerly entitled to take fees from those who made applications to them. As I pointed out, the first stipendiary magistrates counted as such by virtue of being paid from public funds as an alternative to this. The alternative seemed desirable, as the fees-system, at least in the county of Middlesex in the eighteenth century, was held to have led to corruption. If lay magistrates were to be paid from public funds, as district judges are, though no doubt very much more modestly, there would be no risk of that kind. (Magistrates' courts continue to charge fees for the discharge of certain functions, notably witnessing declarations, but the money goes to the court – that is, to public funds – and not to any individual). The question therefore seems not to be one of principle, but rather to be the practical one of whether lay justice would work better if the magistrates were paid. I can think of only one respect in which that might be claimed with any plausibility, which is that of recruitment: are there people who would make effective justices who do not apply for appointment simply or mainly because they would be unpaid?

In the nature of the case, it is hard to say if there are many such people, but I believe it to be most unlikely. Most applicants for appointment seem to be prompted by the anticipated interest of the work and by a wish to fill a social role – also perhaps by a consideration which was certainly strong in the past, that of enhancing their social status. Taken together, these motivations seem quite strong enough to draw out enough applications for the appointment-process to be fairly selective. None of them is financial in character, and it is not at all obvious that a purely financial motivation, distinct from the first two I have mentioned, is one which we would gain from encouraging.

It should be remembered in considering this that lay magistrates are already entitled to claim expenses and that this extends to compensation for loss of pay, though not necessarily to the full reimbursement of what may have been lost. The question is not one of a choice between money and no money at all.

For my own part, I welcomed the fact that I was unpaid. It was at least one strong distinguishing feature which marked off what I did from the work of a *fonctionaire*. I had been an employed person as a civil servant and had had too much of that role to wish to return to it. Beyond this, there is the practical point that, least of all at the present time (2015), no government would wish to incur additional expenditure in circumstances where there is no demand for it. I have hardly ever heard a justice of the peace complain about working for nothing. If payment is so far outside the range of the likely, it is hardly worth discussing further. I will however return to the point in my concluding chapter, where I will modify slightly the conclusion I have just offered.

13.

A Radical Solution

I have concluded that the present constitution of the magistracy, lay and professional, is broadly acceptable as it is – the conclusion of the Morgan-Russell Report – and, second, that the lay magistracy might be made more effective with some changes, which need not be radical, in its selection and training, along with a more positive attitude on the part of central government. In this chapter I will set out an alternative to the *status quo* which is more far-reaching. In doing so, I retract nothing of what has gone before. What I will now describe is an alternative to something which is broadly – if only broadly – adequate. It is not therefore proposed out of a sense of urgency, as if to something clearly not good enough.

The change would be, to start by putting it simply, the amalgamation of the lay magistracy with the stipendiary magistracy, now the district judiciary, which emerged from it some two hundred years ago. There would be a single magistracy, sitting in benches of three, exceptionally of two, made up both of persons legally qualified and of others not so qualified, and so organised that the chair was always taken by one of the qualified. As the legal advice needed by those not qualified would be provided by the chair-taker, it would no longer be necessary to have the services of a legally qualified clerk.

It has always been possible for stipendiary magistrates/ district judges to sit with lay magistrates, and it is sometimes, though only rarely, arranged that they should. One such occasion was the trial, some ten years ago, of Sir Stephen Richards, a member of the Court of Appeal. He was charged with indecent assault. It must have been obvious that such an arrangement would be preferable to the trial of a very senior judge being before another judge sitting solo. It must also have seemed preferable to a trial before a lay bench; I have remarked already on the unliklihood of a lay bench being assigned cases which have attracted much publicity. What I am now suggesting is that it is not only in such unusual cases as this that a bench of the kind I have described will be preferable.

Here is a radical proposal, but hardly a surprising one: it must have occurred to many people. There are objections to each of the alternative ways of constituting the tribunal for the purposes of summary justice. They will have occurred to readers of this book, and would have occurred to the hypothetical observers introduced in the first chapter. The obvious objection to the district judge sitting solo, as sole judge of law and fact, and with sole responsibility for sentence, is that this represents a judicial dictatorship which is found nowhere else in the criminal justice system. In the Crown Court, judges sit solo on the bench but with a jury to deliver the verdict in disputed cases; in the Court of Appeal and above, judges sit in benches of at least two. It therefore seems to be for those who would justify the *status quo* to take up the burden of proof. The fact that the present arrangement is so rarely criticised can be attributed to long habituation. It has indeed the decided merit of being cheap (it is also brisk, which makes for cheapness, but briskness seems to me a rather doubtful merit). It could indeed be made even cheaper; district judges sit with legally qualified clerks, though they cannot really need to.

I need say any more about the demerits of the existing alternative to district judges sitting solo – that is, a tribunal composed of lay magistrates. The whole of this book will have made those apparent. I have already said that I do not take them to be a decisive objection to the *status quo*, while accepting some criticisms and indicating possible improvements. Nonetheless, it is a good test of one's real view of any problematic situation to imagine oneself as part of the action, not merely an observer. I often wondered, during my time on the bench, what my informed preference would be if I were myself to be charged with a criminal offence of the kind dealt with by magistrates. Would I wish to appear before a lay bench or before a district judge? A little reflection was enough to bring out the difficulty of answering such a question: what sort of lay bench? I could not be unaware how far these differed in capacity. District judges offered a greater uniformity, but this might be one of case-hardened obtuseness. What I came to appreciate was that the answer would depend on whether or not I had acted unlawfully as charged and – not the same thing – how I would plead. Obtuseness, whether professional or lay, might be to my advantage. My conclusion was however usually that the ideal tribunal would be the one I am now recommending: one with a district judge in the chair and a lay magistrate on either side. It was only such a tribunal, I came to feel, that would do me justice according to the law if my defence were one which relied on a fair degree of legal subtlety. The fear that a lay bench advised by a clerk might not take fully on board what might be a complicated submission, with some fine verbal distinctions, is what led me to the conclusion which I am now offering, that amalgamating the professional and lay components of the magistracy would enhance its competence.

My record of a part of a day in court shortly before I retired seems relevant:

'After lunch, the trial of a driver for touting for hire without a licence. The defendant is present and represented; the CPS is not ready – one of two police witnesses, the only one available, is engaged elsewhere and will be late. We are therefore asked to adjourn briefly. This is opposed, and we refuse. The prosecutor then applies to put in the record of interview [with the defendant, by the police]. This is opposed, both as being 'out-of-time' and on its merits. Some protracted argument, which makes me feel – again – that a tribunal uninstructed in the law of evidence, and barely instructed in criminal procedure more generally, is not up to dealing with the points raised. We turn, of course, to the clerk who scurries off to consult and research. The question is one of the admission of hearsay evidence and of its admission 'out-of-time' i.e. without notice. The court *may*, we are advised, dispense with the obligation to give notice and should be guided by the over-riding concern to do justice. We decide, therefore, to allow the application 'out-of-time' and then decline [reject] it, having been referred to the case of Picton. This suggests, it seems, that we shouldn't admit hearsay in this form just to save the prosecution from the consequences of its incompetence. So, no evidence can be offered and we dismiss the charge, with costs to the defendant.

'This was, and I've no reason to think otherwise, a satisfactory outcome, but I went off sharply aware of my limitations. Very weary'. (2008)

This is the sort of experience which lies behind the recommendation I am now making. I do not want to overstate the arguments for it, but the rough-and-readiness of the process I have recorded will be apparent.

What I am now proposing finds a parallel in a report, presented by Lord Justice Auld in 2001, entitled *Review of the Criminal Courts of England and Wales*. One of its comprehensive proposals was the establishment of a criminal court with jurisdiction between the Crown Court and magistrates' courts, both of which would have continued as they were. The proposed court would have been composed of lay magistrates with a judge in the chair, normally a district judge but, when there were special reasons, by one more senior. Its sentencing powers would have been a lot wider than those of the magistrates' courts of 2001 or today. This proposal was not accepted – or has not yet been accepted – and I refer to it here only to show that my own comparable proposal is no great novelty.

The procedure adopted in the Richards case could be adopted without legislation. In that case the clerk to the 'mixed' bench was legally qualified, as are all magistrates' clerks. It is a legal requirement that a lay bench should sit only with such a clerk to advise it. The law would need to be modified to remove the requirement, leaving the district judge in the chair as the sole source of legal advice. This would, I believe, be necessary, both in order to obtain the cost-saving which is part of the appeal of my proposal and to ensure that there were not conflicting sources of legal advice to the lay members of the tribunal.

To sum up: if what I am recommending were to come about, there would continue to be lay and unpaid magistrates, who for the sake of continuity might continue to be called justices of the peace, and also district judges, who would continue to be salaried, who might or might not continue to be so styled. No one would take the chair in a magistrates' court without being legally qualified and no one would sit alone. A clerk would continue to be needed to deal with points of administration, as Crown Court clerks, not legally qualified, do already, but would not give legal advice. The bench would take its law from the professional in the chair.

This is a simple and conservative proposal. It offers a solution, appropriate to the present day, to a problem which has run with the lay magistracy since its inception. I refer the reader to Chapter Eight, where I remark on the institution of the *quorum*. It is not a proposal which could be brought into effect overnight, as it would take time to assemble an adequate number of chair-takers. That is hardly an objection. If the *status quo* is broadly acceptable, as I have argued it is, its supersession over a period – say ten or fifteen years – should be tolerable, indeed barely noticeable. I offer no costing of what I have proposed, as there are too many uncertainties for this to be worth doing, but it will be obvious that it would require many more paid magistrates. It would also permit the replacement of legally qualified advisors, over the same period and at the same pace. There can be little doubt that, taking the two changes together, there would be an additional charge to public funds.

What I have described would, I have no doubt, be decidedly unpopular. While I believe it would be to the benefit of the public, and therefore probably welcome to that part of the public which took it on board, it would almost certainly be unwelcome to most members of the three classes of people immediately concerned. District judges would, I suspect, dislike it on the understandable ground that sitting as one of three, even if in the chair, would be a diminution of their autonomy. It would indeed be. Those used to sitting alone would have to get used to sitting as one of three, with the possibility of being voted down by the other two on questions of fact or sentencing. They would probably be irritated by the increase in the time required to dispose of a day's list, which would come about with the need to consult. One can think of other objections. Lay magistrates, for the most part, would be less immediately and directly affected. Most obviously, they would need to get used to taking advice on points of law, which would now amount to directions, from a legally qualified chair-taker and not from a clerk. This should not be difficult. In an earlier chapter, I brought out the way the way in which the stipendiary magistracy emerged from the ranks of the justices of the peace of eighteenth century Middlesex. It would now be necessary for the lay magistracy to recognise a process of re-absorption rather than of take-over.

What I have described and am now proposing could only be unwelcome to the present Justices' Clerks and their legally qualified staff. Their role would simply be abolished. If, however, the reconstruction were to be brought about only gradually, as it would have to be, the adverse consequences for those affected would be considerably mitigated. In particular, legal advisors of the right calibre could expect to be strong candidates for appointment as chair-takers, and so salaried, to the new amalgamated bench.

In dealing with the consequences for lay magistrates, I did not mention what might be the most unwelcome change of all. This is that lay magistrates would no longer be able to look forward to taking the chair in court – in effect, directing proceedings. For many lay magistrates, this is one of the main attractions of the job, making it much more demanding but also more satisfying. I certainly found it more satisfying. It may therefore be argued, against what I have described, that one of its consequences would be that some of the most useful lay magistrates would be lost, and that candidates with that ambition would not apply for appointment. I think there is much force in this contention; it fastens on what I take to be the strongest objection to what I have described. Many lay magistrates who now take the chair are adequate or more than adequate in the role, and it would be argued, against what I have described, that it would be absurd to take the role away from those who had discharged it well over a period.

That last point could be very largely met by bringing the new arrangement into effect only gradually, as it would have to be.

The point that there would be an adverse effect on recruitment to the lay bench remains. It could be met by a small modification to what I have just proposed. This would be to permit lay magistrates with a certain length of experience, perhaps eight years, to qualify to take the chair on passing an examination in criminal law and procedure. Such people would, after a fashion, be legally qualified, though only in that area of the law with which they would be directly concerned. I believe that this degree of qualification, together with an appreciable period of doing the day-to-day work of the bench, would normally be quite enough to prepare them for the demands of the chair and for the guidance of their colleagues in the retiring room.

There would be little difficulty in setting up arrangements for the examination of aspirant chair-takers. Until it became a requirement for legal advisors to be barristers or solicitors, it was possible to qualify for the job by taking a course at a polytechnic (as it then was) and obtaining a certificate in magisterial law. The modification I have just described would, in one light be a limited reversion to that arrangement.

I now conclude. What I have suggested here and in the last chapter would, I believe, have a strengthening and revivifying effect on a longstanding national institution. I have tried to show how adaptable the magistracy has proved to be and, especially, how much it has changed over the past sixty years. This gives every ground for expecting that it could easily accommodate the modest and conservative proposals made here, should they be found persuasive.